FIXING YOUR FINANCES ONE STEP AT A TIME

GIVE ME CREDIT FOR TRYING

Shelton Marchman

GMCFT Publishing

Published by GMCFT Publishing

ISBN (Paperback): 978,1,7373688,0,9

ISBN (eBook): 978,1,7373688,1,6

First Edition, 2026

Printed in the United States of America

GiveMeCreditForTrying.com

Disclaimer: This book is for informational and educational purposes only. It does not constitute financial, legal, or professional advice. Please consult a qualified professional before making financial decisions.

My Dedication Page

To Maggie, Preston, Ava and Maximus, thank you for always being my support system. Win, lose or draw, every day is the best day with you guys in my corner.

TABLE OF CONTENTS

INTRODUCTION: BEFORE WE BEGIN

November 12, 2011 changed everything.

A drunk driver named Will ran a red light at 80 miles per hour and T,boned the passenger side of my car at the intersection of Route 40 and Route 896 in Newark, Delaware. Heading South, thinking he was going North to Philadelphia 45 minutes away. Three broken ribs. Three fractured vertebrae. A separated shoulder. A broken clavicle, torn meniscus in both knees. Nerve damage and glass embedded in my face, arms, and head.

My son had wanted to watch the fight with me that night. Thank God he didn't. His football team had won the championship game so he spent the night with his friends. He would've died that night and I almost did.

But here's what didn't show up in the medical reports, the crash that nobody saw coming was the one that happened to my finances.

Before Will, I was comfortable. I paid my bills on time. I had decent credit. I thought I had time to get everything in order. Eighteen months of surgeries, recovery, and no income destroyed all of it. The collectors started calling me, the scripts I had written were being repeated verbatim to me on the phone. I had spent over a decade running collections for multiple multi,million dollar lending portfolios. If it wasn't rent, insurance, electricity or groceries, it was an option to pay. I maxed out three credit cards and borrowed as much as I could. I picked up side work helping mortgage loan officers settle debts for clients that couldn't close with the negative credit on their reports. I was furious. This wasn't my fault. WILL did this to me.

Seven months after the accident, I pulled a one,inch piece of glass out of my own arm in the shower, one of many pieces the doctors said my body would push out on its own eventually because surgically removing them would have done more damage than good since they were so deeply embedded. Something shifted. I realized that even when the glass is gone, the pain remains. Will had changed my life permanently. But it was my choices going forward that would determine my future.

Slowly I built my **CHAOS** system ,**Changing Habits to Advance Our Situation**.

This book is not a theory. It was forged in the worst eighteen months of my life. It was tested by someone who had collectors calling while managing credit risk for a living. It was refincd over twenty years of helping people navigate financial devastation,through divorce, job loss, medical emergencies, and bad decisions, and come out the other side.

The eighteen chapters ahead are not steps toward perfection. They are steps toward progress. And progress starts with one decision: to stop fighting your chaos and start using it.

You don't need everything figured out. You don't need perfect credit, a clean budget, or a clear plan. You just need to be willing to begin.

That's all I had after that shower. That and the hope that I could do it by trying my best. And it was enough.

Give yourself credit for trying.
— Shelton Marchman

Chapter 1: Meet CHAOS

In an instant, a drunk driver named Will shattered my life—destroying my car, my body, and leaving me with a MAJOR financial setback for 18 months of little to no income. Yet, from that devastation, I unearthed an unforeseen gift: the ability to see a way to turn chaos into success at any level.

What if your financial turmoil isn't an adversary, but an untapped wellspring of potential? The **CHAOS** system—Changing Habits to Advance Our Situation—emerged from a genuine crisis and has been forged in the crucible of financial recovery. This isn't an abstract theory from someone untouched by financial hardship; it's a proven method, battletested, for transforming your darkest financial moments into your most remarkable comeback.

Whether you're navigating a crisis or simply weary of financial stress dictating your life, **CHAOS** meets you when and where you are. Perfection, impeccable organization, or having all the answers aren't prerequisites. You only need to be willing to begin anew and harness it as a tool. By the conclusion of this book, you'll possess the tools to convert any financial chaos into structured progress toward the life you genuinely desire.

CHAOS: A True Definition

You've experienced chaos, but you've never truly understood it. Allow me to clarify.

CHAOS, contrary to Webster's definition of "a state of utter confusion" (which paints it as an adversary), is actually an opportunity in disguise. I keep myself motivated with acronyms that change my thinking to motivate myself in low points. This situation was CHAOS and I wanted to own the chaos. I came up with Changing Habits to Advance Our Situation.

This isn't just a clever acronym; it's the system that transformed my life at the time, rebuilt my finances, and taught me to convert any catastrophe into progress.I've used the same process to mitigate anything that pops up ever since. When Will assaulted me, I tailspinned into a mental and physical that required a re-wire. I learned that my life goes on for everyone even if it's standing still for me. By learning to manage the chaos rather than be consumed by it, I was able to put things back together piece by piece.

Why Most People Stay Stuck

Here's what happens to most of us when chaos hits: We try to control it. We fight against it. We exhaust ourselves trying to make the chaos go away so we can get back to "normal."

But here's the truth, there is a NEW normal. Life is chaotic. Your finances are chaotic. Your job situation changes. Your family needs a shift. Your health fluctuates. The economy moves up and down.The normal you knew prior to your situation is gone. Chaos isn't the exception; it's the rule.

The people who succeed aren't the ones who avoid chaos. They're the ones who learn to use it to motivate themselves to grow.

Your Current **CHAOS**

Before we go any further, let's identify what we're working with. What chaos is currently disrupting your financial life? (i.e.divorce,death in the family, job loss, etc.)

Your Top 5 Financial Challenges Right Now:

☐ Challenge 1: ______________________________

☐ Challenge 2: ______________________________

☐ Challenge 3: ______________________________

☐ Challenge 4: ______________________________

☐ Challenge 5: ______________________________

Don't overthink this. Write down whatever financial stress keeps you awake at night, whatever money problem makes your stomach tighten, whatever financial situation makes you feel powerless.

These aren't character flaws. These aren't permanent sentences. These are simply your current chaos, and chaos is workable.

Finding your Will

Will was my wake-up call, I could've done without him crashing into me but here we are! Your "Will" might be:

- Living paycheck to paycheck despite working overtime
- Credit card debt that keeps growing no matter what you do
- A job that doesn't pay enough for the life you need to live
- An emergency that wiped out your savings
- Student loans that feel like a life sentence
- A divorce that destroyed your financial foundation

Whatever brought you to this book, whatever **CHAOS** you're facing—that's your **WILL**. And just like my Will, your chaos contains the seeds of your transformation.

The **CHAOS** Promise

By the end of this book, you'll have a complete system for turning financial chaos into organized progress. You'll know exactly how to:

- Change the habits that keep you financially stuck
- Habits that advance your situation instead of holding you back
- Advance toward the financial future you actually want
- Our situation—because this affects everyone you care about

- Situation into something you're proud of and excited about

This isn't about perfection. This isn't about never having problems again. This is about building the skills to handle whatever chaos comes next and using it to get stronger. To grow mentally and physically.

SUMMARY:

- Chaos isn't your enemy—it's raw material for transformation
- Everyone has a "WILL" that can become their turning point
- The CHAOS system turns disorder into organized progress
- Your current financial challenges are workable, not permanent

Your Next Step: Identify your top 5 financial challenges. We'll use these throughout the book to apply each CHAOS principle to your specific situation.

Chapter 2: What is YOUR WILL?

When Chaos Finds You

November 12, 2011. I'll never forget that date, because that's when I learned what real chaos looked like.

I was driving home from watching the Pacquiao/Marquez fight at my friend Dave's place, sober as a judge. Earlier that day, I'd watched my son, Preston,win his little league football championship. He'd thought about coming to watch the fight with me, but chose to celebrate with his team instead. Thank God he did.

Will was 45 minutes from home in Newark, Delaware, celebrating Homecoming at his alma mater. He'd been drinking ALL DAY LONG. Now he was behind the wheel, traveling 80 mph on a 45 mph road, going the wrong direction, further away from Philadelphia instead of toward it.

I met Will at the intersection of Route 40 West and Route 896 South.

"He never even tapped the brake."

Those words still haunt me. An off-duty officer who witnessed the crash said Will was doing 80 mph easily when he ran the red light and destroyed the passenger side of my car, the side Preston would have been sitting on.

The door collapsed so far that I was about two inches from the door handle. I was thrown across the car. I hit my head on the front window so hard that I shattered it and then ricocheted down and partially under the passenger dashboard. My legs were still wedged under the steering wheel. Three broken ribs, three fractured vertebrae, a separated shoulder, broken clavicle and torn meniscus in both knees. Sprinkle in the nerve damage in my wrist, and shards of glass embedded in my head, arms, and face and you're reading the medical catastrophe that was my chart. Will T,boned me at 80 MPH and crushed me.

I was blessed to live and MORE BLESSED that Preston wasn't with me.

The Crash After the Crash

The physical injuries were just the beginning. The real crash happened to my finances and my personal life. Time has taught me that Will has forever impacted me, but it's my choices today that will determine my future.I can keep replaying the accident and hating Will or I can make a plan to move forward day by day.

Will gave me the anger. But it was up to me to take responsibility for my growth.

Finding Your Will

You don't need a drunk driver to slam into you before you take control of your situation. But something brought you to this book. Something made you realize that your current financial path and plan isn't taking you where you want to go.

Your Will might be:

The Sudden Crisis:

- Job loss that revealed how little you had saved
- Medical emergency that destroyed your budget
- Divorce that split your financial foundation
- Emergency repair that maxed out your credit cards

The Slow Realization:

- Years of living paycheck to paycheck despite good income
- Watching friends buy homes while you're stuck renting
- Realizing retirement is approaching with no savings
- Credit card debt that keeps growing despite minimum payments

The Breaking Point:

- Being denied for a loan you thought you'd qualify for
- Your child asking for something you can't afford
- Lying awake at night worried about money
- Feeling trapped by your financial situation

The Biggest Lesson From Will

Here's what I eventually realized: I needed Will.

Not the pain, not the injuries, not the financial devastation. But I needed the wake-up call. I needed something big enough to shake me out of my assumption that I had unlimited time to figure things out.

Will forced me to confront a hard truth: I had put myself in a position to fall by not building better money habits into my life. I had assumed life would continue as it was. I hadn't planned for **CHAOS**.

My financial decline happened quickly after the accident, but the habits that made it possible had been building for years. The crash just exposed the weakness that was already there.

Your Wake-Up Call

Take a moment to identify your Will:

What specific event or realization made you face your financial situation?

____

How long has the underlying problem been building before you recognized it?

____

What would happen if you don't change anything in the next year?

____

What are you most afraid of financially?

____

What do you want your financial story to be one year from now?

____

The Choice

Will threw me into chaos, but he also gave me a choice: Stay angry and stuck, or use that energy to rebuild better than before.

You have the same choice. Your Will,whatever brought you here, can be the beginning of your financial transformation or just another problem you complain about.

The chaos is already here. The question is: What are you going to do with it?

SUMMARY:

- Your "Will" is whatever forced you to face your financial reality
- Crisis often exposes weaknesses that were already there
- The same event that creates chaos can fuel your transformation
- You get to choose whether chaos destroys you or builds you up

Your Next Step: Identify your specific "Will" and write down what you want your financial story to look like one year from now. This becomes your North Star for the **CHAOS** system.

Chapter 3: Reflecting on Your Own CHAOS-Where Are You and How Did You Get Here?

Taking Inventory

Now that you've met your Will and identified what brought you here, it's time for an honest assessment. This isn't about judgment or shame, it's about getting clear on your starting point so you know exactly what you're working with.

Think of this like a financial GPS. You can't get directions to your destination until the system knows your current location. Right now, we're finding your coordinates.

Your Current Reality

Let's start with the big picture. If you had to describe your current financial situation in one word or phrase, what would it be?

My financial situation right now is: ____________________________________

Be honest. Is it "struggling," "treading water," "embarrassing," "out of control," or something else entirely? Whatever comes to mind first is probably the most accurate.

Is this acceptable to you? If you're reading this book, probably not. And that's exactly where we need to start,with the acknowledgment that where you are isn't where you want to stay.

The Ripple Effect

Your finances don't exist in a vacuum. They touch every part of your life, every relationship, every decision you make. Let's map out how your current money situation is affecting the rest of your world.

How is your current financial situation affecting your life?

Your stress levels:

____

Your relationships:

____

Your daily decisions:

____

Your sleep: ____

Your future plans:

____

What you can't do right now because of money:

____

The Future You're Heading Toward

If nothing changes, if you keep the same habits, same spending patterns, same approach to money, where will you be in:

1 year: ____

5 years: ____

10 years: ____

Is that future acceptable? Does it scare you? Good. Fear of staying the same is one of the most powerful motivators for change.

How You Got Here: The Positive Forces

Before we look at what went wrong, let's acknowledge what's gone right. Even in financial chaos, there are strengths and positive forces that got you this far. These are the assets we'll build on.

What are the benefits and positives in your past?

- Skills that come naturally to you:

  ____

- People who have helped you: ____________________________________
- Good financial habits you already have:

  ____

- Times you successfully overcame challenges:

  ____

Don't skip this section. Your transformation will be built on your existing strengths, not just fixing your weaknesses.

The Negative Forces: Your Financial "Glass Shards"

Just like I had glass embedded in my body that worked its way out over time, you probably have financial "glass shards",negative events, bad habits, or limiting beliefs that are still affecting you.

What specific events have affected you negatively?

- Financial setbacks or crises: ____________________________________
- Bad financial advice you followed:

  ____

- Money mistakes you made: ____________________________________

What emotions did you take away from those events? Are you letting those emotions hold you down, or can you use them to build you up?

____

What habits do you currently have that are hindering your progress?

- Daily spending habits: ____________________________________
- How you handle money stress:

  ____

- Financial decisions you avoid making:

  ____

When did you develop these habits and why?

____

The Root Cause

Most financial problems aren't really about money,they're about the deeper issues money represents. Let's dig into yours.

What causes you the most stress in your life?

____

What's the root cause of this stress? ___________________________________

When did it begin? ___________________________________

Do you feel like you have control over this aspect of your life?

____

The Most Important Question

This last question might be the hardest, but it's the most important for everything that follows:

Do you want to change?

Not "Do you wish things were different?" Everyone wishes that. But do you want to try every day to improve your current situation, knowing it will be difficult and require sacrifices? Do you want something better enough to do the work?

Your answer: ____

If your answer is anything less than a strong "yes," stop here. Come back to this book when you're ready to commit to the process. Change requires energy, and half,hearted effort leads to half,hearted results.

If your answer is yes, then let's get clear on what you're working toward.

What Do You Actually Want?

What do you want out of life financially?

Think about this as specifically as you think about your coffee order. You wouldn't walk into Starbucks and say, "I want something caffeinated that tastes good." You know exactly how you like your coffee.

You should know your financial goals just as clearly.

In 1 year, I want my finances to look like:

____

In 5 years, I want to be earning: ___________________________________

In 10 years, I want to have saved: ___________________________________

The financial stress I most want to eliminate is:

____

The financial freedom I most want to gain is:

____

Your Chaos Assessment Complete

You now have a clear picture of:

- Where you are financially and emotionally
- How you got here (both positive and negative forces)
- Where you're headed if nothing changes
- What you actually want instead
- Your commitment level to making changes

This assessment becomes the foundation for everything we build next. In the following chapters, we'll use the CHAOS system to bridge the gap between where you are and where you want to be.

SUMMARY:

- Honest assessment is the starting point for all change
- Your finances affect every area of your life
- You have both strengths to build on and obstacles to overcome
- Knowing what you want is as important as knowing what you don't want
- Change requires genuine commitment, not just wishful thinking

Your Next Step: Review your answers above. Circle the three responses that surprise you most or feel most urgent. These will be your priority areas as we move into the **CHAOS** framework.

Chapter 4: Bad Finances Are Like an Abusive Relationship

The Toxic Partnership

Imagine being trapped in the worst relationship you've ever witnessed. Your partner constantly makes you feel inadequate, withholding affection and gaslighting you into thinking everything is your fault. On bad days, you don't want to get out of bed. There's always tension when you're together, but guilt and self-doubt when you're apart.

Other people whisper behind your back but never say anything directly,they don't want to get involved. They can't see how bad it really is because you've gotten so good at hiding it.

That's exactly what bad finances feel like.

The Invisible Prison

Your financial problems are invisible to most people, which makes them both easier to hide and harder to escape. You can drive a nice car (financed), live in a decent place (barely affording rent), and maintain social appearances while drowning privately.

Just like an abusive relationship, bad finances:

Control Your Decisions

- You can't take the job you want because you need the higher salary
- You can't move to a better place because you can't afford deposits
- You can't help family members because you're barely helping yourself

Isolate You From Opportunities

- You avoid social situations that cost money
- You don't network because you can't afford to reciprocate invitations

- You turn down experiences that could improve your life

Damage Your Self-Worth

- You feel like a failure when loan applications are denied
- You believe you're not disciplined enough to manage money
- You think you don't deserve financial stability

Create Constant Stress

- You check your bank balance with dread
- You avoid opening bills
- You lie awake calculating and recalculating expenses

The Comfortable Lie

Here's the most dangerous part: Just like staying in a toxic relationship, it's tempting to accept bad finances because leaving feels scarier than staying.

The False Safety of Financial Dysfunction:

"At least I know what to expect." You've learned to manage the chaos. You know which bills you can pay late, which credit cards have room, which expenses you can put off. Change feels risky.

"What if I try and fail?" Better to stay in familiar misery than risk the embarrassment of attempting change and not succeeding.

"People might judge me." If you start shopping at thrift stores, cooking at home instead of eating out, or driving an older car, others might see your real financial situation.

"I can't afford to change." This is the biggest lie. You can't afford NOT to change, but the immediate cost of transformation feels overwhelming compared to the slow burn of staying the same.

The Hidden Costs of Staying

But just like an abusive relationship, bad finances don't stay stable—they get worse over time.

The Downward Spiral:

Year 1: You're managing. Using credit cards for emergencies, paying minimums, telling yourself it's temporary.

Year 3: The minimums are harder to make. You're borrowing from one card to pay another. Stress is affecting your sleep and relationships.

Year 5: You're avoiding calls from creditors. Your credit score has tanked. Friends are pulling away because you always decline invitations.

Year 7: You've lost opportunities for better jobs because of credit checks. Your marriage is strained by constant money fights. Your health is suffering from chronic stress.

Year 10: You're financially trapped. Can't get loans for anything. Can't retire. Can't help your children. Living entirely paycheck to paycheck despite years of income.

The Breaking Point

Remember my glass shard moment? That piece of glass working its way out of my shoulder months after the crash? That's what financial rock bottom feels like—the moment when pretending everything is fine becomes more painful than facing the truth.

Your breaking point might be:

- Being declined for a loan you desperately needed
- Realizing you have nothing saved for your child's education
- Your spouse discovering debt you've been hiding
- Having to choose between medication and groceries
- Facing retirement with no savings

The Choice: Leave or Stay

You have the same choice I had after Will crashed into my life: Use this chaos to rebuild, or stay trapped in the wreckage.

Leaving the Financial Abuse Means:

Short-term Pain

- People might notice you spending less
- You'll have to say no to things you used to say yes to
- You'll face uncomfortable conversations about money
- You'll have to change habits that feel comfortable

Long-term Freedom

- Sleeping peacefully without money anxiety
- Making decisions based on what you want, not what you can afford
- Having options instead of feeling trapped
- Building a legacy instead of just surviving

Breaking Free Requires Support

Just like leaving an abusive relationship, escaping financial dysfunction is easier with help. You need:

Your Financial Support Team:

- Someone who will hold you accountable to your goals
- Someone who understands your situation without judgment
- Someone who will celebrate your wins and encourage you through setbacks
- Someone who has successfully made similar changes

This might be a spouse, friend, family member, or financial counselor. The key is having someone in your corner who wants your success more than they want you to stay comfortable.

The CHAOS Intervention

This is where the **CHAOS** system becomes your intervention strategy—your planned escape from financial dysfunction.

Just like leaving an abusive relationship requires:

- Courage to admit the situation isn't working

- Honest assessment of what needs to change
- Action plan for creating safety and stability
- Outside support from people who care about you
- Steady commitment to the new path even when it's difficult

The **CHAOS** system requires:

- Changing the habits that keep you trapped
- Habits that advance your situation instead of destroying it
- Advancing toward financial freedom step by step
- Our situation, including everyone who's affected by your financial health
- Situation that you control instead of one that controls you

Your Intervention Moment

Right now, today, you get to choose: Stay in this toxic financial relationship, or commit to the work of getting free.

The relationship is over when you decide it's over.

Not when your debt is paid off. Not when you get a better job. Not when you have more money saved. The abusive relationship with your finances ends the moment you stop accepting that this is just how things are for you.

Your Declaration:

"I am no longer willing to let bad finances control my life, my relationships, my decisions, or my future. I commit to learning and practicing the habits that will advance my situation, no matter how uncomfortable the process becomes."

Sign and date: ____

SUMMARY:

- Bad finances function like an abusive relationship,controlling, isolating, and damaging
- Staying feels safer than changing, but the situation always gets worse over time
- Breaking free requires support, commitment, and a clear action plan
- The CHAOS system is your intervention strategy for financial freedom
- The relationship ends when you decide it ends—not when circumstances change

Your Next Step: Identify your financial support team. Who will you ask to support your transformation? Contact them this week and share your commitment to change.

Chapter 5: GPS , Goal, Plan, Success

Your Financial Navigation System

When I decided to rebuild my life after Will, I realized I needed more than good intentions. I needed a system as reliable as the GPS on my phone,something that could guide me from where I was to where I wanted to be, with clear directions and the ability to recalculate when I got off track.

That's when I developed what I call my **FINANCIAL GPS.**

GOALS- PLAN-SYSTEM

Just like your phone's GPS, this system requires three things:

- **GOAL**: Your destination (where you want to be financially)
- **PLAN**: Your route (the specific steps to get there)
- **SUCCESS**: Your arrival confirmation (how you'll know you've made it)

Goal: Setting Your Financial Destination

You can't get directions without a destination. Yet most people approach their finances like they're just driving around randomly, hoping to end up somewhere good.

The Coffee Shop Test

Remember how quickly you can order your coffee? "Large iced chai latte with a shot of espresso, to go." No hesitation. No menu studying. You know exactly what you want.

You should be able to describe your financial goals with the same clarity and speed.

Your Financial Goals (Be Specific):

1 Year Goal: By [specific date], I will have:

- Saved: $________
- Paid off: $________
- Monthly income of: $________

- Debt reduced to: $________

5 Year Goal: By [specific date], I will have:

- Net worth of: $________
- Annual income of: $________
- Emergency fund of: $________
- Major debt status: ____

10 Year Goal: By [specific date], I will have:

- Retirement savings of: $________
- Passive income of: $________
- Financial independence level: ____
- Legacy goal: ____

If you can't fill these in immediately, you're not ready to start changing your finances. You're just hoping things get better. Hope isn't a strategy.

Make Your Goals SMART:

- Specific: "Save money" → "Save $5,000"
- Measurable: "Pay off debt" → "Pay off $15,000 in credit card debt"
- Achievable: Based on your actual income and expenses
- Relevant: Connected to what you actually want in life
- Time,bound: "Someday" → "By December 31, 2026"

Plan: Your Step,by,Step Route

Once you know where you're going, you need to map out how to get there. Your plan breaks down big goals into manageable daily and weekly actions.

The Monthly Breakdown Method:

Take your 1year savings goal and divide by 12. If you want to save $6,000 in one year, you need to save $500 per month.

Take your debt payoff goal and divide by months. If you want to pay off $12,000 in credit cards over 2 years, that's $500 per month in extra payments.

Your Monthly Action Plan:

To reach my 1,year goals, I need to:

- Save $_______ per month
- Pay extra $_______ toward debt per month
- Increase income by $_______ per month
- Reduce expenses by $_______ per month

The Weekly Breakdown:

Monthly savings ÷ 4 = $_______ per week to save Monthly debt payment ÷ 4 = $_______ per week extra toward debt

The Daily Breakdown:

Weekly target ÷ 7 = $_______ per day I need to save or redirect toward debt

Your Daily Habits Plan:

To save/redirect $_____ per day, I will:

- Skip: ___________________ (saves $_____)
- Choose instead: ___________________ (saves $_____)
- Earn extra by: ___________________ (earns $_____)

Example Daily Habits:

- Skip the $5 coffee shop visit → Make coffee at home (saves $5)
- Choose generic brands → Instead of name brands (saves $2,3/day)
- Pack lunch → Instead of buying lunch (saves $8,12/day)
- Walk/bike → Instead of Uber for short trips (saves $10,15/ride)

Success: How You'll Know You've Arrived

Success isn't just reaching your financial numbers—it's fundamentally changing your relationship with money and chaos.

Financial Success Markers:

Level 1: Stability (Months 1-6)

- You check your bank balance without anxiety
- You pay all bills on time without stress
- You have $1,000 emergency fund
- You track your expenses automatically

Level 2: Progress (Months 6-18)

- Your debt is decreasing every month
- Your savings are growing consistently
- You make financial decisions based on your plan, not emotions
- You handle unexpected expenses without panic

Level 3: Control (Months 18-36)

- You have 3,6 months of expenses saved
- You invest regularly for long,term goals
- You help others with financial advice
- Money stress rarely keeps you awake at night

Level 4: Freedom (3+ years)

- You make career decisions based on fulfillment, not just money
- You give generously without financial strain
- You have multiple income streams
- You're building generational wealth

Life Success Markers:

The real success isn't just numbers,it's how your improved finances change your life:

- Relationships improve because money stress decreases

- You sleep better and have more energy
- You take opportunities instead of just surviving
- You model financial health for your family
- You have options instead of feeling trapped

GPS Recalculation: When You Get Off Track

Just like your phone's GPS, your Financial GPS needs to recalculate when you take a wrong turn or hit unexpected obstacles.

Monthly GPS Check-in:

☐ Am I on track to hit my monthly savings target?

☐ Did I stick to my spending plan 80% of the time?

☐ What obstacles came up that I didn't plan for?

☐ What's working better than expected?

☐ What needs to be adjusted for next month?

Quarterly Route Adjustment:

Every 3 months, review and adjust:

- Are my goals still realistic and relevant?
- Has my income or situation changed?
- What lessons have I learned about my spending patterns?
- Do I need to speed up or slow down my timeline?

The Power of GPS Thinking

The GPS mindset changes everything:

- Instead of: "I'm bad with money" → "I'm learning the route"
- Instead of: "I'll never get out of debt" → "I'm 23% of the way to my destination"
- Instead of: "I messed up this month" → "GPS is recalculating my route"

Your financial transformation isn't about perfection,it's about consistent navigation toward your chosen destination.

SUMMARY:

- GPS (Goal, Plan, Success) provides clear navigation for financial change
- Goals must be as specific as your coffee order
- Plans break down big goals into daily actionable habits
- Success has multiple levels and includes life improvements beyond money
- Regular check,ins and adjustments keep you on track

Your Next Step: Complete your GPS worksheet above. Set specific 1-year, 5-year, and 10-year goals, then calculate your monthly and daily action requirements.

Chapter 6: When You Stumble , GPS Recalculation

The Inevitable Detour

Here's what no one tells you about financial transformation: You will get off track. Not might—will.

You'll have the month where an emergency wipes out your progress. You'll have a week where you abandon your budget completely. You'll have the day where you make every financial mistake you swore you'd never make again.

This isn't failure. This is part of the journey.

When your phone's GPS recalculates after you miss a turn, it doesn't say, "You idiot! You've ruined the entire trip!" It calmly says, "Recalculating route," and gives you new directions from exactly where you are.

Your Financial GPS works the same way.

Common Financial "Wrong Turns"

The Emergency Setback Your car breaks down, and the repair costs $1,200. You have to use money earmarked for debt payment or drain your small emergency fund.

The Emotional Spending Binge You have a terrible week at work, fight with your spouse, and spend $400 on things you don't need because it temporarily makes you feel better.

The Social Pressure Override Your friends plan an expensive weekend trip. You know you can't afford it, but you go anyway because you don't want to be left out or explain your financial situation.

The Income Disruption Your hours get cut at work, your freelance client doesn't pay on time, or your side hustle income drops unexpectedly.

The Success Sabotage You're making great progress, so you "reward" yourself with purchases that undo months of hard work.

The Two Types of GPS Recalculation

Type 1: External Chaos (Not Your Fault)

- Medical emergencies
- Job loss or hour reduction
- Car repairs or home maintenance
- Economic downturns
- Family crises requiring financial help

Type 2: Internal Chaos (Your Choices)

- Emotional spending
- Abandoning your budget
- Making purchases to avoid difficult conversations
- Procrastinating on important financial tasks
- Returning to old spending habits

Both types are workable, but they require different approaches.

External Chaos: The Emergency Protocol

When external chaos hits, your GPS needs emergency mode, a stripped-down version that focuses on survival and damage control.

Emergency Financial GPS:

1. Stop the bleeding: What's the minimum needed to handle this crisis?
2. Triage your goals: Which financial goals pause temporarily while you handle this?
3. Protect the foundation: What core financial habits must you maintain no matter what?
4. Plan the recovery: How will you get back on track once this crisis passes?

External Chaos Example: Sarah's car needs $1,800 in repairs. She has $500 in emergency savings and was paying $300/month extra toward credit cards.

Emergency GPS Recalculation:

- Use $500 emergency savings + put $1,300 on credit card for repairs
- Pause extra debt payments for 3 months
- Maintain minimum payments and basic savings habits
- Resume debt acceleration once emergency fund is rebuilt ($300/month for 2 months)
- This delays her debt-free date by 5 months, but she stays on track overall

Internal Chaos: The Choice Protocol

When internal chaos strikes, when you make choices that derail your progress, you need a different approach focused on learning and recommitment.

Choice Aftermath GPS:

1. Acknowledge without shame: "I made choices that moved me away from my goals."
2. Analyze the trigger: What situation or emotion led to these choices?
3. Identify the pattern: When have I made similar choices before?
4. Adjust the plan: How can I handle this trigger differently next time?
5. Recommit to the route: What's my next right financial decision?

Internal Chaos Example: Mike had a terrible performance review at work and spent $600 on electronic gadgets to feel better. This was money he planned to put toward his emergency fund.

Choice Protocol:

- Acknowledge: "I used spending to cope with work stress."
- Analyze: "I felt like a failure and wanted to feel successful at something, even if it was just buying things."
- Pattern: "I do this whenever I feel criticized or inadequate."
- Adjust: "Next time I feel this way, I'll call my accountability partner and go for a walk instead of going to the store."

- Recommit: "I'll return what I can and restart my emergency fund savings this week."

The 24-Hour Reset Protocol

Sometimes you need immediate GPS recalculation. Here's your 24-hour financial reset process:

Hour 1: Stop and Assess

- What exactly happened?
- How much did it cost/set me back?
- Was this external chaos or internal chaos?

Hours 2-6: Damage Control

- What can I return or cancel?
- What bills/payments can I adjust this month?
- Who do I need to contact about changed circumstances?

Hours 7-12: Emotional Processing

- If this was internal chaos, what was I really trying to accomplish?
- If this was external chaos, what emotions am I dealing with?
- Who can I talk to for support and perspective?

Hours 13-24: Route Recalculation

- What's my new timeline for my original goals?
- What do I need to change about my daily habits?
- What's my next right financial decision?

The Power of Negative Emotions

Remember: Negative emotions aren't the enemy of financial progress, they're fuel for it, when used correctly.

Anger as Fuel

- Instead of: "I'm angry at myself for spending $400 on stupid stuff"
- Try: "I'm angry enough at this situation to make sure it never happens again"

Fear as Motivation

- Instead of: "I'm scared I'll never get out of debt"
- Try: "I'm scared enough of staying in debt that I'll do whatever it takes to change"

Frustration as Clarity

- Instead of: "I'm frustrated that this is so hard"
- Try: "I'm frustrated enough to find a better system that works for me"

Building Anti-Fragile Finances

The goal isn't to avoid all setbacks, it's to build finances that get stronger from setbacks. This is what I call "anti-fragile" finances.

Anti-Fragile Financial Habits:

- Multiple small emergency funds instead of one large one
- Automatic savings that adjust with your income
- Flexible debt payment plans that can pause and resume
- Skills that let you earn extra income when needed
- Support systems that help you recover from setbacks quickly

Your Stumble Recovery Plan

When I inevitably get off track financially, I will:

1. My 24-hour reset contact person: ______________________________________ (Someone I can call immediately for support and accountability)

2. My emergency financial protocol: ________________________________ (What gets paused, what continues, what gets prioritized)
3. My choice recovery process: ________________________________ (How I'll analyze and learn from internal chaos)
4. My recommitment ritual: ________________________________ (What I'll do to get back on track and stay motivated)

The GPS Promise

Your Financial GPS will recalculate as many times as necessary. There is no number of wrong turns that makes your destination unreachable. There is no setback that's too big to recover from. There is no mistake that disqualifies you from financial success.

The only way to fail is to stop using the GPS entirely.

SUMMARY:

- Everyone gets off track,setbacks are part of the journey, not evidence of failure
- External chaos requires emergency protocols; internal chaos requires choice analysis
- Negative emotions can fuel financial progress when channeled correctly
- Anti-fragile finances get stronger from setbacks instead of weaker
- GPS recalculates as many times as needed, the destination doesn't change

Your Next Step: Create your personal Stumble Recovery Plan. Write down your contact person, emergency protocol, and recommitment process. Keep this somewhere easily accessible for when you need it.

Part 3: Embrace the CHAOS

"Chaos isn't something that happens to you—it's raw material you can shape into whatever you choose to build."

Chapter 7: Organized Chaos is Your Friend

Making Peace with Disorder

I live most of my life in chaos. My wife jokes that at least it's *organized* chaos. She's right,I've learned to work with disorder instead of fighting against it.

Here's what I discovered after Will crashed into my life: You can't eliminate chaos, but you can absolutely harness it. The same energy that destroys can be redirected to build. The same unpredictability that creates problems can be channeled to create solutions.

Most people exhaust themselves trying to control chaos. They want perfect budgets, perfectly organized finances, and perfectly predictable outcomes. When chaos inevitably appears, they feel defeated and give up entirely.

I'm going to teach you a different approach: Organized Chaos.

What Chaos Really Is

Traditional Definition: Chaos is disorder, randomness, unpredictability. It's the drunk driver hitting you at 2 AM. It's your carefully organized plans falling apart. It's standing still while the world happens around you.

CHAOS Definition: Changing Habits to Advance Our Situation. Chaos becomes the energy source for transformation instead of the obstacle preventing it.

The difference isn't in what happens to you, it's in how you respond to what happens to you. You can't let chaos break you.

The Chaos Mindset Shift

Old Mindset: "Why do bad things keep happening to me? I can't catch a break. Nothing ever goes according to plan."

CHAOS Mindset: "Chaos is information. Chaos shows me where my systems need to be stronger. Chaos gives me energy for change."

When your car breaks down unexpectedly:

- **Old:** "This always happens at the worst time. I can't afford this."
- **CHAOS**: "This shows me I need a bigger emergency fund and a more reliable vehicle. What habits can I change to make that happen?"

When you overspend on groceries:

- **Old:** "I have no self-control. I'm terrible with money."
- **CHAOS:** "This shows me my meal planning system needs work. What habits can I build to shop more strategically?"

The Secret Power of Chaos

Here's what most people miss: Chaos is incredibly motivating when you stop trying to control it and start using it.

Chaos Creates Clarity When everything is falling apart, you quickly discover what actually matters. The emergency strips away all the non,essential spending and focuses you on true priorities.

Chaos Builds Strength Just like physical exercise creates controlled damage that makes muscles stronger, financial chaos can build your money management muscles when you respond strategically.

Chaos Reveals Truth When systems break down, you see where the real problems are. Chaos exposes weaknesses you could fix and strengths you didn't know you had.

Chaos Generates Energy Nothing motivates change like the discomfort of staying the same. Chaos makes staying in your current situation feel more painful than doing the work to change.

My Organized Chaos System

After my accident, I had to rebuild everything. Instead of trying to create a perfect, controlled financial life, I built systems that could handle chaos and get stronger from it.

The Four Pillars of Organized Chaos:

1. Flexible Structure

Instead of rigid budgets that break under pressure, create flexible frameworks that bend without breaking.

- Emergency protocols for when income drops
- Scalable savings that adjust with your situation
- Multiple small goals instead of one big goal that failure destroys

2. Rapid Response Systems

Instead of detailed plans that become useless when chaos hits, develop rapid response capabilities.

- 24-hour financial reset protocols
- Emergency decision,making frameworks
- Quick ways to generate extra income when needed

3. Anti-Fragile Habits

Instead of habits that only work in perfect conditions, build habits that get stronger under pressure.

- Automatic savings that you don't have to think about
- Multiple income streams that protect against job loss
- Simple tracking systems that work even during crazy times

4. Chaos Conversion Protocols

Instead of being defeated by setbacks, systematically convert chaos into progress.

- Every financial crisis teaches you something about your systems
- Every mistake becomes data for improving your processes
- Every setback reveals new strengths and capabilities

Organized Chaos in Action

Traditional Approach to Job Loss: Panic → Use credit cards to maintain lifestyle → Hope to find new job quickly → Go deeper into debt → Feel defeated and hopeless

Organized Chaos Approach: Immediate spending reduction → Activate emergency protocols → Network for opportunities → Use time between jobs to build new skills → Emerge stronger with better job and improved financial systems

Traditional Approach to Unexpected Expense: Stress about the money → Put it on credit card → Promise to pay it off later → Make minimum payments → Feel guilty about debt → Avoid dealing with finances

Organized Chaos Approach: Assess the expense → Use emergency fund if available → If not available, create plan to pay it off quickly → Use this as motivation to build bigger emergency fund → Emerge with better preparation for next time

The Chaos Advantage

People who learn to work with chaos instead of against it have significant advantages:

Adaptability: They handle change better because they expect it and plan for it.

Resilience: Setbacks don't defeat them because they've built systems designed to handle setbacks.

Opportunity Recognition: They see possibilities in disruption that others miss.

Stress Tolerance: They're calmer during crises because chaos feels familiar and workable.

Innovation: They create unique solutions because they're not trapped by conventional thinking.

Your Chaos Assessment

What chaos are you currently fighting instead of harnessing?

What would change if you saw this chaos as energy for transformation?

What systems in your life break down under pressure?

What would anti-fragile versions of these systems look like?

Embracing Your Chaos Nature

Maybe you're not naturally organized. Maybe you don't like detailed budgets and complex financial planning. Maybe your life is just inherently chaotic because of work, family, health, or other circumstances.

Good. That means you're perfectly positioned to use the Organized Chaos approach.

Instead of fighting your nature, we're going to work with it. Instead of trying to eliminate chaos from your life, we're going to organize it into a force for positive change.

The most successful people I've worked with aren't the ones who avoid chaos, they're the ones who get comfortable dancing with it.

SUMMARY:

• Chaos can't be eliminated, but it can be harnessed as energy for transformation • Organized Chaos builds flexible systems that get stronger under pressure • The goal is anti,fragile finances that improve through challenges • Your chaotic nature is an advantage, not a problem to fix • CHAOS = Changing Habits to Advance Our Situation

Your Next Step: Identify one area where you're fighting chaos instead of organizing it. Write down how you could build an anti,fragile system for this area instead.

Chapter 8: Changing , Overcoming the Fear of Change

The Evolution Problem

We're perfectly evolved to fear change. For thousands of years, anything new or different could kill us. New foods might be poisonous. New territories might have predators. New situations meant uncertainty, and uncertainty meant danger.

Our brains still work this way. When you think about changing your spending habits, part of your brain screams: "Danger! Unknown outcome! Stay safe! Keep doing what you've been doing!"

This fear of change isn't a character flaw, it's ancient wiring designed to keep you alive. But what once protected us now traps us.

The Modern Change Paradox

Today, the biggest danger isn't change,it's staying the same.

Staying the same financially means:

- Your debt grows while your income stagnates
- Inflation erodes your purchasing power
- You miss opportunities while others advance
- Your problems compound while solutions remain untried

But your brain doesn't see it that way. Your brain sees:

- Current situation = known and survivable (even if miserable)
- Changed situation = unknown and potentially dangerous

The Hidden Fears Behind Financial Paralysis

Most people think they're just "bad with money" or "not disciplined enough." Really, they're afraid of specific things that come with change:

Fear of Judgment "What will people think if I stop going out as much?" "What if friends notice I'm shopping at thrift stores?" "What if my lifestyle changes make others uncomfortable?"

Fear of Failure

"What if I try to change and it doesn't work?" "What if I sacrifice now and still don't reach my goals?" "What if I'm just not capable of being good with money?"

Fear of Success "What if I actually succeed and then people expect more from me?" "What if having money changes who I am as a person?" "What if success creates pressure I can't handle?"

Fear of Loss "What if I give up things I enjoy and feel deprived?" "What if being responsible with money makes my life boring?" "What if I save money and then something happens to it?"

The Change Conversation

Here's the conversation happening in your head when you think about financial change:

Logical Brain: "I need to stop eating out so much and save that money."

Fear Brain: "But what if you're invited out and have to say no? People might stop inviting you. You could become socially isolated. What if you're missing important networking opportunities? What if the one time you say no to dinner is when someone was going to offer you a job?"

Logical Brain: "That's probably not going to happen."

Fear Brain: "Probably not. But it COULD happen. And you know what definitely WON'T happen? You won't die if you keep ordering takeout. You've survived this long. Why risk it?"

Logical Brain: "Because my credit card debt keeps growing."

Fear Brain: "That's tomorrow's problem. This restaurant decision is today's problem. Play it safe."

Sound familiar? This internal negotiation happens dozens of times per day, usually without you realizing it.

Confronting Fear with Logic

The solution isn't to eliminate fear,it's to respond to fear with information instead of avoidance.

Fear Response: "I can't change my spending because I don't know what will happen."

Logic Response: "I can research what actually happens when people make these changes. I can talk to people who've done it successfully. I can make small changes first to test the outcomes."

Fear Response: "What if people judge me?"

Logic Response: "Some might. But the people who judge me for making responsible financial choices aren't people whose opinions I should value. The people who matter will respect my goals."

Fear Response: "What if I fail?"

Logic Response: "Failure is not permanent. If something doesn't work, I can try a different approach. The only real failure is never trying to improve my situation."

The Change Ladder

Instead of jumping into massive changes that trigger maximum fear, use the Change Ladder, small steps that build confidence and prove change is safe.

Rung 1: Information Gathering

- Read about others who've made similar changes
- Calculate the actual costs of staying the same
- Research the specific benefits of the changes you're considering

Rung 2: Experimental Changes

- Try the change for one week as an experiment
- Make reversible changes first
- Change one small thing while keeping everything else the same

Rung 3: Supported Changes

- Tell someone about your change plan for accountability
- Find others making similar changes
- Get help with implementation

Rung 4: Systematic Changes

- Build the change into your routine
- Create systems that make the change automatic
- Track results to prove the change is working

Rung 5: Identity Changes

- See yourself as someone who successfully makes positive changes
- Help others make similar changes
- Use this success to tackle bigger changes

Change Example: The Latte Factor

Fear Brain Scenario: "I spend $5/day on coffee. I should make coffee at home instead." Fear Response: "But I love that coffee! It's my one pleasure! Making coffee at home is so much work! What if the home coffee tastes terrible? What if I'm grumpy without my good coffee and it affects my work? What if I save the money but then spend it on something worse?"

Change Ladder Approach:

Rung 1: Research how much $5/day actually costs annually ($1,825). Research good home coffee methods. Find others who've made this change successfully.

Rung 2: Experiment for one week. Buy good coffee and a decent coffee maker. Track mood and energy to see if there's any real difference.

Rung 3: Tell a friend about the experiment. Set up automatic transfer of the $5/day savings to a separate account where you can watch it grow.

Rung 4: Build home coffee,making it into a morning routine. Track the growing savings account. Calculate progress toward larger financial goals.

Rung 5: Help a friend make a similar change. Use this success as proof that you can change other spending habits too.

The Fear Antidote: Knowledge and Community

Knowledge Defeats Abstract Fear The more specifically you understand what you're afraid of and why, the more you can address those fears directly.

Instead of "I'm scared to change my spending," identify: "I'm scared that if I spend less on entertainment, I'll lose touch with friends who like expensive activities."

Now you can solve that specific problem: "I can suggest cheaper alternatives when friends want to do expensive things. I can budget for occasional splurges. I can find new friends who share my financial goals."

Community Defeats Isolation Fear Find others who are making similar changes. Online communities, local groups, accountability partners,connect with people who understand what you're going through and have succeeded at similar transformations.

Your Change Fear Inventory

What specific changes do you know you need to make?

What exactly are you afraid will happen if you make these changes?

How realistic are these fears? What evidence do you have for and against them?

What information could you gather to address these fears?

What small experimental change could you try for one week?

Who could support you through this change?

The Change Commitment

Change becomes easier when you realize that NOT changing is actually the riskier choice.

Your current financial trajectory,if nothing changes, leads to a predictable outcome. Are you willing to accept that outcome for the rest of your life?

If not, then change isn't optional. It's necessary.

The question isn't whether change is scary. The question is: What scares you more, the discomfort of changing, or the consequences of staying the same?

SUMMARY:

- Fear of change is evolutionary wiring that now works against us
- Most financial paralysis comes from specific, addressable fears
- The Change Ladder makes large changes feel manageable and safe
- Knowledge and community are the most effective fear antidotes
- NOT changing is actually the riskier choice long,term

Your Next Step: Complete your Change Fear Inventory above. Choose one small change to experiment with for one week. Focus on gathering evidence about what actually happens when you change, rather than what you fear might happen.

Chapter 9: Habits - The Building Blocks of Transformation

Your Life is Your Habits

Right now, as you're reading this, you're demonstrating dozens of habits. How you're sitting, where you chose to read, when you decided to pick up this book, how you hold it, where your eyes move on the page, all habits.

You probably brushed your teeth this morning without thinking about it. You likely took the same route to work you always take. You probably checked your phone within the first hour of waking up. You made coffee or tea the same way you made it yesterday.

Here's the profound truth: Your life is nothing more than the sum of your habits.

Your financial situation is the sum of your money habits. Your health is the sum of your eating and exercise habits. Your relationships are the sum of your communication and attention habits. Your career is the sum of your work and learning habits.

This is simultaneously the most depressing and most hopeful truth about human behavior.

Depressing: If your habits are creating results you don't want, then your current trajectory is probably going to continue unless you change something fundamental.

Hopeful: If you can change your habits, you can change your entire life. And habits, unlike personality or circumstances, are completely within your control.

The Anatomy of a Habit

Every habit has three components: Trigger → Action → Reward

Trigger: The cue that starts the habit. This can be a time (7 AM), a place (kitchen), an emotion (bored), another habit (after I brush my teeth), or a person (when my spouse comes home).

Action: The behavior itself. This is what most people focus on when they're trying to change habits, but it's actually the least important part.

Reward: What you get from doing the habit. This can be physical (caffeine), emotional (feeling productive), social (connection with others), or psychological (sense of completion).

Example: The Morning Coffee Habit

- Trigger: Waking up + walking to the kitchen
- Action: Making coffee + drinking it
- Reward: Caffeine energy + feeling ready to start the day + comfort ritual

Example: The Debt,Creating Shopping Habit

- Trigger: Feeling stressed + seeing an online sale notification
- Action: Browsing shopping websites + making purchases
- Reward: Temporary distraction from stress + excitement of getting packages + feeling like you're treating yourself well

Why Habit Change Feels Impossible

Most people fail at changing habits because they focus only on the Action part and ignore the Trigger and Reward.

Common Mistake: "I need to stop spending money on clothes." Why It Fails: You're trying to eliminate the Action without addressing why you start shopping (Trigger) or what you're really trying to get from shopping (Reward).

Better Approach: "I shop when I'm stressed because it temporarily makes me feel better. I need to find a different way to handle stress that gives me the same sense of treating myself well."

The Four Types of Financial Habits

Type 1: Automatic Money Habits

These happen without conscious thought and usually involve small amounts that add up over time.

Examples:

- Buying coffee every morning ($1,500/year)
- Ordering delivery instead of cooking ($2,400/year)
- Buying things in checkout lines ($300/year)
- Subscription services you forgot about ($480/year)

Change Strategy: Make the bad habit harder and the good habit easier.

Type 2: Emotional Money Habits

These happen in response to feelings and often involve larger amounts.

Examples:

- Shopping when stressed or sad
- Expensive nights out when celebrating
- Impulse purchases when feeling deprived
- Lending money when feeling guilty

Change Strategy: Address the underlying emotion while finding healthier ways to get the same reward.

Type 3: Social Money Habits

These happen in response to social situations and pressure from others.

Examples:

- Going to expensive restaurants because friends suggest them
- Buying clothes to fit in with coworkers
- Spending on activities to avoid explaining your financial situation

- Gift,giving beyond your means

Change Strategy: Prepare scripts and alternatives in advance, find a like-minded community.

Type 4: Avoidance Money Habits

These happen because you're avoiding dealing with financial tasks or information.

Examples:

- Not checking account balances
- Paying bills late because you don't want to see the numbers
- Using credit cards to avoid budgeting conversations
- Procrastinating on financial planning

Change Strategy: Make financial tasks as easy and non-threatening as possible.

The Habit Change Playbook

Strategy 1: Habit Stacking (Adding Good Habits)

Attach a new habit to an existing habit that's already solid.

Formula: "After I [existing habit], I will [new habit]."

Examples:

- "After I brush my teeth, I will check my bank balance."
- "After I pour my morning coffee, I will write down yesterday's expenses."
- "After I eat lunch, I will transfer $5 to savings."

Strategy 2: Habit Swapping (Changing Bad Habits)

Keep the same trigger and reward, but change the action.

Current Habit: Bored (trigger) → Online shopping (action) → Entertainment/distraction (reward)

New Habit: Bored (trigger) → Play a mobile game for 10 minutes (action) → Entertainment/distraction (reward)

Advanced New Habit: Bored (trigger) → Work on a creative project (action) → Entertainment/sense of accomplishment (reward)

Strategy 3: Environment Design

Change your environment to make good habits easier and bad habits harder.

Make Bad Habits Harder:

- Delete shopping apps from your phone
- Unsubscribe from promotional emails
- Keep credit cards in a drawer, not your wallet
- Use a different browser for entertainment vs. work

Make Good Habits Easier:

- Set up automatic transfers to savings
- Put healthy financial books where you'll see them
- Use apps that round up purchases and save the change
- Keep a visible thermometer showing debt payoff progress

Strategy 4: The Two,Minute Rule

Any new habit should take less than two minutes to complete.

Don't Start With: "I will create and maintain a detailed budget." Start With: "I will write down one expense every day."

Don't Start With: "I will cook all my meals at home." Start With: "I will prepare one ingredient for tomorrow's breakfast."

Once the two-minute version becomes automatic, you can build it into something bigger.

Your Personal Habit Analysis

Three Good Financial Habits You Already Have:

1. ______________________________

2. ______________________________

3. ______________________________

What makes these habits stick? What are their triggers and rewards?

____

Three Bad Financial Habits You Want to Change:

1. ______________________________

2. ______________________________

3. ______________________________

For each bad habit, identify:

- Trigger: What starts this habit?

  ____

- Action: What exactly do you do?

  ____

- Reward: What do you get from it?

  ____

Building Your First New Habit

Choose ONE financial habit to build using the habit stacking method:

After I [existing solid habit] ______________________________, I will [new financial habit] ______________________________.

Examples:

- After I start my car, I will say my financial goal out loud.
- After I sit down at my computer in the morning, I will check yesterday's spending.

- After I finish dinner, I will put all loose change in a savings jar.

Your Habit Stack: After I ________________________________, I will ________________________________.

The Habit Timeline

Days 1-7: Focus only on doing the habit, not doing it perfectly. The goal is repetition, not results.

Days 8-21: The habit starts to feel more natural. You might miss a day here and there, that's normal. Just get back to it the next day.

Days 22-66: The habit becomes more automatic. You start to feel weird when you don't do it. This is when you can start optimizing or building on the habit.

Day 66+: Research shows this is the average time for a habit to become truly automatic. Some habits take longer, some shorter, but by this point it should feel natural.

Habit Troubleshooting

"I keep forgetting to do my new habit." Your trigger isn't strong enough. Attach it to a more established habit or create a stronger environmental cue.

"I do the habit sometimes but not consistently." Your habit might be too big. Make it smaller and easier until consistency develops.

"I was doing great but then stopped completely." This is normal. Just restart. Don't try to "make up" for missed days—just begin again with the next occurrence of your trigger.

"The habit feels pointless because it's so small." Small habits compound over time. Trust the process. A 1% improvement every day leads to 37x improvement over a year.

The Habit Multiplier Effect

Here's the magic of financial habits: They don't just change your money—they change your identity.

When you consistently check your bank balance, you become "someone who is aware of their finances."

When you consistently save small amounts, you become "someone who prioritizes their future."

When you consistently make conscious spending decisions, you become "someone who is in control of their money."

This identity change is what makes all other financial improvements possible.

SUMMARY:

- Your financial life is the sum of your financial habits
- Every habit has three parts: Trigger → Action → Reward
- Focus on changing triggers and rewards, not just actions
- Use habit stacking, environment design, and the two,minute rule
- Start with one small habit and build consistency before expanding
- Habits change your identity, which changes everything else

Your Next Step: Choose one habit stack from your analysis above. Commit to doing it for 7 days straight, focusing only on consistency, not perfection.

Chapter 10: Advance , Moving Forward with Purpose

The Difference Between Motion and Progress

After Will crashed into my life, I spent months in motion but made very little progress.

I was busy—doctor appointments, physical therapy, insurance calls, legal meetings. I was moving constantly, but I wasn't advancing toward anything meaningful. I was just reacting to whatever demanded my attention that day.

Motion is activity without direction. It's being busy without being effective. It's changing things without improving them.

Progress is purposeful movement toward a specific goal. It's a strategic activity that builds on itself over time. It's making choices that compound into the future you actually want.

Most people are in constant motion with their finances—paying bills, checking balances, worrying about money, making purchases—but they're not advancing toward financial freedom. They're just managing financial chaos instead of organizing it into progress.

The Advance Mindset

To advance means to move forward with intention. It means you're not just surviving your current situation—you're actively building toward a better one.

Survival Mindset: "How do I get through this month?" Advance Mindset: "How does this month move me closer to my 5-year goal?"

Reactive Approach: "I need to deal with this financial problem." Advance Approach: "How can I solve this problem in a way that prevents it from happening again?"

Scarcity Thinking: "I can't afford to make any changes right now." Advance Thinking: "I can't afford NOT to make changes that will improve my future position."

The Four Pillars of Financial Advance

Pillar 1: Strategic Thinking

Every financial decision serves your larger strategy or works against it. There are no neutral financial choices.

Questions for Strategic Thinking:

- How does this spending decision advance my financial goals?
- What will this choice cost me in opportunity over 5 years?
- Am I solving this problem or just postponing it?
- What would the financially successful version of me do in this situation?

Example: You need a car repair that costs $800. Survival Response: Put it on a credit card, worry about it later. Strategic Response: Use emergency funds if available. If not available, this reveals I need a bigger emergency fund AND a more reliable car. Create a plan for both.

Pillar 2: Compound Habits

Small actions that build on themselves over time create exponential results.

Daily Advance Habits:

- Check account balances (builds awareness)
- Record expenses (builds consciousness)
- Save/invest something, even $1 (builds wealth,building identity)
- Learn one financial concept (builds knowledge)
- Practice one money skill (builds capability)

Weekly Advance Habits:

- Review and adjust spending for the coming week
- Evaluate progress toward monthly goals
- Research one way to increase income or decrease expenses
- Connect with others who share your financial goals

Monthly Advance Habits:

- Full financial review and GPS recalculation
- Analyze what worked and what didn't in the past month
- Set specific goals and actions for the coming month
- Invest time in building new income streams

Pillar 3: Skill Development

Your earning power and financial intelligence are your most important assets. Advancing means consistently building both.

Financial Skills to Develop:

- Budgeting and cash flow management
- Debt elimination strategies
- Investment basics and portfolio building
- Tax planning and optimization
- Negotiation (for salary, bills, purchases)
- Side hustle development

Career Advancement Skills:

- Industry,specific technical skills
- Leadership and communication abilities
- Networking and relationship building
- Personal branding and reputation management
- Problem,solving and innovation capabilities

The Learning Compound Effect: Every skill you develop makes learning the next skill easier. Every increase in capability makes future advances more achievable.

Pillar 4: Network Building

Your financial success is significantly influenced by the people around you. Advancing means intentionally building relationships with others who are also moving forward.

Your Financial Network Should Include:

- Accountability Partners: People committed to similar financial goals
- Mentors: People who've achieved what you're working toward
- Peers: People at similar stages who can share struggles and strategies
- Students: People you can teach and help (teaching reinforces your own learning)

Network Advance Activities:

- Join financial wellness groups or online communities
- Attend industry meetups and professional development events
- Find a mentor or coach who's achieved your goals
- Become a mentor to someone a few steps behind you

The Advance Action Framework

Daily Advance (5-10 minutes)

Morning: Review your financial goals and choose one action that advances them today. Evening: Record the day's financial decisions and their alignment with your goals.

Weekly Advance (30-45 minutes)

Review: How did this week advance your financial position? Plan: What three actions will advance your goals next week? Learn: Study one financial topic or skill for 15 minutes.

Monthly Advance (2-3 hours)

Analyze: Full financial review using your GPS system. Adjust: Modify goals or strategies based on what you've learned. Advance: Choose one new area to focus on improving next month.

Quarterly Advance (Half day)

Assess: Major review of all financial goals and progress. Strategize: Plan major moves for the next quarter. Invest: Dedicate significant time to skill building or network development.

Advance in Different Life Areas

Career Advancement

Immediate (This Month):

- Update your resume and LinkedIn profile
- Have a career conversation with your manager
- Apply for one stretch assignment or opportunity
- Connect with one new person in your industry

Short-term (This Quarter):

- Develop one new skill relevant to your career goals
- Attend one industry event or conference
- Start a side project that showcases your abilities
- Build relationships with three people who could influence your career

Long-term (This Year):

- Position yourself for promotion or new role
- Build expertise that makes you indispensable
- Create multiple income streams
- Develop leadership abilities

Relationship Advancement

Financial Relationships:

- Have honest money conversations with your spouse/partner
- Find an accountability partner for your financial goals
- Join communities of people with similar financial values
- Distance yourself from people who encourage poor financial habits

Professional Relationships:

- Build relationships with people one level above you professionally
- Maintain connections with peers in your field
- Mentor someone who's earlier in their career
- Develop relationships with potential business partners or collaborators

Personal Development Advancement

Knowledge Building:

- Read financial and career development books regularly
- Take courses that build valuable skills
- Stay current with trends in your industry
- Learn from successful people's strategies and mistakes
- Use AI to teach you as a mentor

Health and Energy:

- Maintain physical health to support mental performance
- Build stress management skills for handling financial pressure
- Develop time management systems that create space for advancement
- Practice delayed gratification and impulse control

Your Personal Advance Plan

Immediate Advance Opportunities (Next 30 Days)

Financial:

1. ______________________________
2. ______________________________
3. ______________________________

Career:

1. ______________________________
2. ______________________________
3. ______________________________

Personal/Skills:

1. ______________________________
2. ______________________________
3. ______________________________

Strategic Advance Goals (Next 90 Days)

What three changes would most significantly advance your situation?

1. ______________________________
2. ______________________________
3. ______________________________

Annual Advance Vision

Where do you want to be one year from today?

Financially: ____

Professionally: ____

Personally: ____

In terms of capabilities:

____

The Advance Accountability System

Daily Check-in: What did I do today to advance my situation?

Weekly Review: What evidence do I have that I'm moving forward?

Monthly Assessment: How has my situation measurably improved?

Quarterly Evaluation: Am I advancing fast enough to reach my annual goals?

Common Advance Obstacles

"I Don't Have Time"

Reality Check: You have time for what you prioritize. Advancing your situation should be a higher priority than entertainment, social media, or other discretionary activities.

Solution: Start with 5 minutes daily. Prove to yourself that small consistent efforts create results.

"I Don't Know What to Do Next"

Reality Check: Perfect knowledge isn't required for progress. You need clarity on direction and willingness to learn as you go.

Solution: Choose one area to focus on for 30 days. Get better at that one thing before trying to improve everything at once.

"I'm Not Seeing Results Fast Enough"

Reality Check: Real advance happens over months and years, not days and weeks. Most people quit just before their efforts would have paid off.

Solution: Track leading indicators (actions you take) not just lagging indicators (results you get). Celebrating process wins, not just outcome wins.

"I Keep Getting Distracted by Urgent Things"

Reality Check: Urgent things will always compete with important things. If you don't protect time for advancement, it won't happen.

Solution: Schedule advancement activities like appointments. Treat them as non-negotiable commitments to your future self.

The Compounding Power of Advance

Here's what most people miss: Every area you advance makes every other area easier to advance.

Financial progress gives you more resources to invest in career development. Career progress increases your income and ability to build wealth. Skill development makes you more valuable professionally and financially. Network building creates opportunities in all other areas. Health improvement gives you energy and clarity for all other advances.

This is why the **CHAOS** system focuses on advancing our situation, not just your individual situation. Every improvement you make benefits everyone connected to you and creates momentum for further improvements.

Summary:

• Advance means purposeful progress toward specific goals, not just motion

• Strategic thinking, compound habits, skill development, and network building are the pillars of advancement

• Daily, weekly, monthly, and quarterly advance activities build systematic progress • Advancement in any area makes advancement in other areas easier

• Consistency over time creates compound results that seem impossible in the short term

Your Next Step: Complete your Personal Advance Plan above. Choose one immediate financial advance action and one career advance action to complete this week. Schedule time for both as non,negotiable appointments with your future self.

Chapter 11: Our (positive feedback), Building Your Support Team

You Are Not Alone in This Fight

During the darkest period of my recovery, when medical bills were piling up and I couldn't work, I felt completely isolated. The constant doctor's appointments and frustrations of daily life wore me down but I didn't want to burden everyone who cared about me with my struggle because I felt like I should have been able to do it alone. I thought I had it figured out, that asking for help was admitting failure.

That isolation almost destroyed me.

The breakthrough came when I realized something profound: My physical and financial recovery wasn't just about me. It was about us—my girlfriend (now wife), my son, our future together. When I stopped trying to shoulder this burden alone and started treating it as our shared challenge, everything changed.

Your financial transformation isn't a solo journey, and it shouldn't be. The people who matter in your life are already affected by your financial situation. The question isn't whether your money problems impact others—it's whether you'll invite them to be part of the solution.

The Ripple Effect of Financial Stress

Your financial chaos affects:

Your Immediate Family

- Spouse/partner stress from money arguments and uncertainty
- Children picking up on financial tension and learning unhealthy money patterns
- Family decisions limited by financial constraints
- Dreams and plans postponed indefinitely

Your Extended Relationships

- Friends who adjust their suggestions based on your perceived financial limitations
- Family members who worry about your financial security
- Colleagues who see you stressed and distracted at work
- Anyone who depends on you financially or emotionally

Your Community

- Local economy when you can't participate fully
- Organizations you can't support financially
- Causes you care about but can't contribute to
- People you could help if you were financially secure

The Multiplier Effect of Financial Success

Just as financial problems spread outward, financial improvements create positive ripples:

When you get your finances organized:

- Your stress decreases, improving all your relationships
- Your family feels more secure and can plan for the future
- You become a positive example for others facing similar struggles
- You have resources to help others in meaningful ways
- You contribute more effectively to your community and causes you care about

This is why the **CHAOS** system focuses on Our Situation—because your transformation lifts everyone around you.

Building Your Financial Support Team

Your support team needs four types of people:

1. The Accountability Partner

Role: Keeps you honest about your goals and commitments. Who: Someone with similar financial goals or values who will ask tough questions. What They Do:

- Check in regularly about your progress
- Call you out when you're making excuses
- Celebrate your wins and encourage you through setbacks
- Share their own struggles and victories

How to Find Them: Look for someone who's also working on financial improvement, join online communities, or ask a naturally disciplined friend to partner with you.

2. The Mentor/Guide

Role: Provides wisdom from someone who's already achieved what you're working toward. Who: Someone whose financial journey and values you respect. What They Do:

- Share strategies that worked for them
- Help you avoid mistakes they made
- Provide perspective when you're overwhelmed
- Connect you with resources and opportunities

How to Find Them: Industry professionals, successful people in your network, authors of books you admire, or formal mentorship programs.

3. The Cheerleader/Emotional Support

Role: Provides encouragement and emotional stability during difficult times. Who: Family member, close friend, or partner who believes in your ability to change. What They Do:

- Listen without judgment when you're struggling
- Remind you of your progress when you feel discouraged

- Support your goals even when it means lifestyle changes for them
- Help you maintain perspective during setbacks

How to Find Them: Usually someone already in your life who cares about your wellbeing.

4. The Peer Group/Learning Community

Role: Provides mutual support and shared learning with others at similar stages.
Who: People facing similar financial challenges or working toward similar goals.
What They Do:

- Share strategies and resources
- Normalize the struggle of financial change
- Provide different perspectives on common problems
- Create social pressure to maintain positive changes

How to Find Them: Online communities, local meetups, financial wellness groups, or classes. We even have a support group for our GMCFT family on Facebook!

The Difficult Conversations

Building your support team requires honest conversations that might feel uncomfortable.

With Your Spouse/Partner

The Conversation: "I need to change our financial situation, and I need your support to do it successfully."

What to Discuss:

- Your current financial reality (numbers, debts, income)
- Your goals and timeline for improvement
- What changes they'll need to make or support
- How you'll make decisions together going forward
- What support you need from them specifically

Common Resistance and Responses:

- *"We've tried this before"* → "This time I have a specific system and I'm committed to following it consistently."
- *"I don't want to live like we're poor"* → "I want us to build real wealth instead of just appearing wealthy."
- *"This sounds like it will be no fun"* → "Short,term sacrifice for long,term freedom and much more fun later."

With Your Family

The Conversation: "I'm making some changes to improve our financial security."

What to Discuss:

- Why this matters for the whole family's future
- What changes they might notice (different spending, activities, etc.)
- How this will benefit them in the long run
- What role they can play in helping achieve these goals

With Children: Age-appropriate explanations about making smart money choices and working toward goals as a family.

With Friends

The Conversation: "I'm focusing on improving my financial situation, so I might not be able to do some of the things we usually do together."

What to Discuss:

- Your commitment to the friendship despite lifestyle changes
- Alternative activities that fit your budget
- Your appreciation for their understanding and support
- How they can help you stay committed to your goals

Friend Filter: Pay attention to how people respond. True friends will support your positive changes. People who pressure you to abandon your financial goals aren't acting in your best interest.

Your Team Building Action Plan

Step 1: Identify Your Current Support Network

Who currently supports your financial goals?

___

Who currently works against your financial goals (intentionally or unintentionally)?

___

What gaps exist in your support network?

___

Step 2: Recruit Your Core Team

My Accountability Partner will be: ______________________
When I will ask them: ______________________

My Mentor/Guide will be: ______________________
How I will approach them: ______________________

My Emotional Support person is: ______________________
What I need from them: ______________________

My Peer Group will be: ______________________

How I will find/join them: ______________________

Step 3: Plan Your Conversations

With my spouse/partner, I need to discuss:

1. ______________________
2. ______________________
3. ______________________

With my family, I need to explain:

1. ______________________
2. ______________________

3. ______________________________

With my friends, I need to communicate:

1. ______________________________
2. ______________________________
3. ______________________________

Managing Relationship Changes

When People Don't Support Your Changes

The Skeptics: People who doubt you'll stick with it because you've tried and failed before. Response: Acknowledge their skepticism but ask them to judge your commitment by your actions, not your past attempts.

The Saboteurs: People who actively encourage you to abandon your financial goals. Response: Limit time with these people during your transformation period. Their resistance often comes from their own financial insecurities.

The Guilters: People who try to make you feel bad for not spending money on them or with them. Response: "I value our relationship, but I need to prioritize my financial health right now. Let's find ways to spend time together that work within my budget."

When Your Success Changes Dynamics

As you improve financially, some relationships may shift:

Success Guilt: You might feel guilty about advancing when others aren't. Solution: Remember that your success gives you more capacity to help others. Model positive change instead of hiding your progress.

Relationship Envy: Some people might become jealous of your financial progress. Solution: Stay humble, share your struggles along with your successes, and offer to help others who want to make similar changes.

New Expectations: People might expect you to pick up more expenses as your situation improves. Solution: Be clear about your boundaries. Just because you have more money doesn't mean you should subsidize others' lifestyles.

The Power of Shared Goals

Family Financial Goals: Instead of "I need to get out of debt," try "We're going to build financial security together."

Examples:

- "We're saving for our dream vacation to [destination]"
- "We're working toward buying our own home"
- "We're building an education fund for the kids"
- "We're creating financial independence so we can retire together"

Community Goals: Connect your financial improvement to larger purposes:

- "Getting financially stable so I can donate to causes I care about"
- "Building wealth so I can help family members in emergencies"
- "Achieving financial independence so I can volunteer more time"

Your Support Team Contract

I commit to:

- Being honest about my progress and setbacks
- Asking for help when I need it
- Supporting my team members' goals in return
- Following through on commitments I make to my team

I ask my support team to:

- Hold me accountable without judgment
- Celebrate progress and encourage me through difficulties
- Be patient with lifestyle changes that affect our relationship
- Support my long,term goals even when short,term sacrifices are required

Together we will:

- Check in regularly about progress and challenges

- Share resources and strategies that could help
- Maintain our relationships while respecting financial boundaries
- Create new traditions and activities that align with our values

SUMMARY:

• Financial transformation affects everyone in your life—invite them to be part of the solution

• Your support team needs accountability partners, mentors, emotional support, and peer groups • Honest conversations about your goals and needed support are essential but may be uncomfortable

• Some relationships may change as you advance,this is normal and necessary

• Shared goals and community purposes make individual discipline easier to maintain

• Your financial success gives you more capacity to help others achieve theirs

Your Next Step: Complete your Team Building Action Plan above. Within the next week, have at least one difficult conversation with someone whose support you need for your financial transformation.

Chapter 12: Situation , Creating the Life You Actually Want

Beyond the Numbers

When I started rebuilding after Will crashed into my life, I made a mistake that almost derailed everything: I focused entirely on the financial numbers and forgot about the life I was trying to create.

I became obsessed with paying off debt, increasing income, and building savings. These were important goals, but they weren't the real goal. The real goal was creating a situation, a life,that I was proud to live and excited to wake up to.

Numbers are just tools. Your situation is what you build with those tools.

What Is Your Situation?

Your situation is the total environment of your life:

- How you spend your time
- Who you spend it with
- What you focus your energy on
- What kind of person you're becoming
- What impact you're having on others
- What legacy you're building

Financial health is crucial to your situation, but it's not your situation.

You can have perfect finances and a terrible situation. You can also have modest finances and an incredible situation. The key is alignment between your money and your values, between your financial choices and the life you actually want to live.

The Situation Assessment

Before you can improve your situation, you need to honestly assess your current one.

Your Time Situation

How do you currently spend your time?

Weekday Breakdown:

- Work: _____ hours
- Commuting: _____ hours
- Family time: _____ hours
- Personal development: _____ hours
- Entertainment/relaxation: _____ hours
- Household tasks: _____ hours
- Sleep: _____ hours

Is this how you WANT to spend your time? ____________________

What would you change if money weren't a factor? ____________________

Your Energy Situation

What gives you energy?

____

What drains your energy?

____

How much of your daily energy goes toward things you care about vs. things you feel obligated to do?

____

Your Relationship Situation

Who are the five people you spend the most time with?

1. ______________________
2. ______________________
3. ______________________
4. ______________________
5. ______________________

Are these relationships energizing you or draining you?

____

Who would you spend more time with if your situation were different?

____

Your Growth Situation

What are you learning and how are you growing?

____

What skills are you developing?

____

What kind of person are you becoming?

____

Are you proud of the direction your life is heading?

____

The Gap Between Current and Ideal

Describe your current situation in one paragraph:

Now describe your ideal situation in one paragraph:

What are the biggest gaps between current and ideal?

1. ______
2. ______
3. ______

Which of these gaps are primarily financial? Which are primarily about choices and priorities?

The Four Domains of Your Situation

Domain 1: Work and Career

Current Reality:

- What do you do for work?
- How much time does it consume?
- How does it align with your values and interests?
- How much financial security does it provide?

Ideal Situation:

- What would meaningful work look like for you?
- How would you balance earning and fulfillment?

- What level of financial security would you want from work?
- How would work fit into your overall life design?

The Bridge: What changes in your financial situation would enable you to make better career choices? What career changes would improve your financial situation?

Domain 2: Relationships and Family

Current Reality:

- Who are the most important people in your life?
- How much quality time do you get with them?
- How do financial concerns affect these relationships?
- What relationship needs aren't being met?

Ideal Situation:

- How would you prioritize relationships if money weren't a constraint?
- What experiences would you create with people you love?
- How would you support and contribute to others' lives?
- What kind of family environment would you build?

The Bridge: How would better finances improve your relationships? How would better relationships support your financial goals?

Domain 3: Personal Growth and Contribution

Current Reality:

- What are you learning and how are you developing?
- What causes or communities do you contribute to?
- What legacy are you building?
- How are you making a difference?

Ideal Situation:

- What would you learn and create if you had more resources?

- How would you contribute to causes you care about?
- What would you want to be remembered for?
- What problems would you help solve?

The Bridge: How would financial security enable you to focus more on growth and contribution? How would focusing on growth and contribution improve your financial situation?

Domain 4: Health and Lifestyle

Current Reality:

- How do you take care of your physical and mental health?
- What activities and experiences bring you joy?
- How much time do you have for rest and renewal?
- What lifestyle elements are missing from your life?

Ideal Situation:

- How would you optimize your health and energy?
- What experiences and adventures would you pursue?
- What would a sustainable, joyful lifestyle look like?
- How would you balance productivity with peace?

The Bridge: How do financial constraints limit your health and lifestyle choices? How would better health and lifestyle support your financial goals?

Your Situation Design Process

Step 1: Values Clarification

What are your core values? What matters most to you in life?

1. ______________________________
2. ______________________________
3. ______________________________
4. ______________________________
5. ______________________________

Step 2: Vision Creation

Write a detailed description of your ideal situation 5 years from now. Include work, relationships, lifestyle, growth, and contribution:

____

____

____

____

____

Step 3: Alignment Check

How well does your current financial plan support this ideal situation?

____

What adjustments do you need to make to your financial goals to better align with your life vision?

____

What adjustments do you need to make to your life vision to be realistic about your financial constraints?

____

The Integration Challenge

The most difficult part of situation design is integrating all four domains without compromising what matters most to you.

Common Integration Challenges:

Time vs. Money Trade-offs

- Higher,paying work that requires more hours
- Time,intensive relationships vs. income,generating activities
- Short,term financial sacrifice for long,term fulfillment

Security vs. Adventure Trade-offs

- Safe financial choices vs. exciting opportunities
- Stable income vs. entrepreneurial ventures
- Conservative lifestyle vs. experiences and growth

Individual vs. Community Trade-offs

- Personal financial goals vs. family needs
- Self-care vs. contribution to others
- Independence vs. interdependence

Your Integration Strategy

What trade-offs are you willing to make to create your ideal situation?

____

What trade-offs are you NOT willing to make?

____

How can you minimize conflicts between different areas of your life?

____

Situation Maintenance and Evolution

Your ideal situation isn't a fixed destination—it's an evolving target that changes as you grow and as circumstances change.

Quarterly Situation Review

Questions to ask every three months:

- Is my current situation moving toward or away from my ideal?
- What's working well in my current situation?
- What needs to be adjusted or changed?
- How have my priorities or values shifted?
- What new opportunities or constraints have emerged?

Annual Situation Redesign

Questions to ask every year:

- How has my vision of my ideal situation evolved?
- What have I learned about what actually makes me happy and fulfilled?
- How do I need to adjust my financial and life strategies?
- What new domains or priorities need attention?

Your Situation Action Plan

Immediate Situation Improvements (Next 30 Days)

What three changes could immediately improve your current situation without requiring major financial changes?

1. ______________________________
2. ______________________________
3. ______________________________

Medium-term Situation Building (Next 6 Months)

What changes require some financial adjustment or planning but are achievable in the near term?

1. ______________________________
2. ______________________________
3. ______________________________

Long-term Situation Goals (Next 2-5 Years)

What situation changes require significant financial progress or major life changes?

1. ______________________________
2. ______________________________
3. ______________________________

The Situation Success Metrics

How will you know when your situation is aligned with your values and vision?

Daily Indicators:

- You wake up feeling energized about your day
- Your time is spent mostly on things you find meaningful
- Your relationships are nourishing rather than draining
- You're growing and contributing in ways that matter to you

Monthly Indicators:

- Your financial choices support rather than contradict your life goals
- You're making progress on things that matter to you long,term
- You feel proud of how you're spending your time and energy
- You're building toward something you're excited about

Annual Indicators:

- You wouldn't trade your situation for someone else's
- People you respect admire the life you're building
- You're making a difference in ways that align with your values
- You have the resources to support the people and causes you care about

The Situation Statement

Complete this statement:

"My ideal situation is one where I___________________________________

____

____

____."

"I will know I'm living this situation when

____

____

____

____."

SUMMARY:

- Your situation is the total environment of your life, not just your financial numbers
- True success requires alignment between your money and your values, your financial choices and your life vision
- Situation design involves integrating work, relationships, growth, and lifestyle domains
- Regular review and adjustment keep your situation evolving toward your ideal
- The goal is creating a life you're proud to live and excited to wake up to

Your Next Step: Complete your Situation Design Process above. Write your situation statement and identify your top three immediate situation improvements. These should guide all your future **CHAOS** applications.

Part 4: Applying CHAOS to Your Finances

*"Knowledge without application is just entertainment. The **CHAOS** system only works when you actually use it on real financial challenges."*

Chapter 13: Debt , Your Financial Prison Break

Debt: The Invisible Shackles

Bad debt is like being in an abusive relationship with your own future. Every purchase you make with borrowed money is your future self paying for your current self's wants. Every monthly payment is your current self paying for your past self's decisions.

The most insidious part? Debt makes you feel like you're living well while actually trapping you in a cycle that gets harder to escape the longer it continues.

But here's what I discovered during my own debt crisis: Debt isn't a moral failing or a permanent condition. It's simply a system that's currently working against you instead of for you. And systems can be changed.

The Real Cost of Debt

Most people think about debt in terms of monthly payments. "I can afford the $350/month car payment." But that's not how debt actually costs you.

Debt costs you in five ways:

1. Interest Multiplication

That $15,000 credit card balance at 18% interest becomes $22,500 if you only make minimum payments. You pay $7,500 extra for the privilege of borrowing money.

2. Opportunity Cost

Every dollar going to debt payments is a dollar NOT going to savings, investments, or opportunities that could improve your situation.

3. Stress Tax

Debt creates chronic stress that affects your health, relationships, and decision-making ability. This has real costs in medical bills, relationship problems, and poor choices made under pressure.

4. Option Limitation

Debt reduces your choices. You can't take the lower,paying job you'd love. You can't move to a better area. You can't help family members in crisis. You can't take entrepreneurial risks.

5. Future Theft

Debt steals from your future self. Every payment is money your future self can't use for retirement, travel, helping children, or pursuing dreams.

Applying CHAOS to Debt Elimination

C -Changing Your Debt,Creating Habits

Identify Your Debt Triggers:

- Emotional spending when stressed, bored, or celebrating
- Social pressure to keep up with others' spending
- Convenience purchases that add up over time
- Emergency expenses because you don't have emergency savings
- Income shortfalls covered by credit instead of budget adjustments

Habit Replacement Strategy:

Old Habit: Stressed (trigger) → Online shopping (action) → Temporary relief (reward) New Habit: Stressed (trigger) → 10,minute walk + call a friend (action) → Actual relief + connection (reward)

Old Habit: Bills due (trigger) → Use credit card (action) → Problem postponed (reward)
New Habit: Bills due (trigger) → Check actual available cash + prioritize payments (action) → Real problem,solving (reward)

Your Debt-Creating Habits to Change:

1. ______________________________
2. ______________________________
3. ______________________________

H -Habits That Accelerate Debt Elimination

Daily Debt,Fighting Habits:

- Check your debt balances every morning (builds awareness)
- Transfer any spare cash immediately to debt payments
- Find one small expense to eliminate and redirect to debt
- Visualize your debt,free future for 2 minutes

Weekly Debt-Fighting Habits:

- Review all spending and identify any debt,creating purchases
- Calculate how much interest you paid this week
- Plan next week's spending to avoid new debt
- Celebrate any progress, no matter how small

Monthly Debt-Fighting Habits:

- Apply any extra money (tax refunds, bonuses, gifts) directly to debt
- Negotiate with creditors for better terms if possible
- Review and optimize your debt elimination strategy
- Track your debt,free date and adjust timeline based on progress

Your New Debt-Fighting Habits:

1. ______________________________
2. ______________________________
3. ______________________________

A - Advancing Your Debt-Free Timeline

The Debt Snowball Method: Pay minimums on everything, then attack the smallest balance first.

- Pros: Quick psychological wins, builds momentum
- Cons: May pay more interest overall

The Debt Avalanche Method: Pay minimums on everything, then attack the highest interest rate first.

- Pros: Saves money on interest
- Cons: May take longer to see progress

The Hybrid Method: Combine both strategies for psychology and math.

- Start with one small debt for quick win and confidence
- Then switch to highest interest rate for efficiency

Your Debt Elimination Strategy: Total debt: $__________ Strategy chosen: __________________ Target debt,free date: ______________ Monthly payment plan: $____________ extra toward debt

O -Our Debt-Free Future

Who benefits when you eliminate debt?

- Your spouse/partner (less financial stress, more options)
- Your children (better example, more family resources)
- Your extended family (you can help instead of needing help)
- Your community (you can contribute instead of just surviving)
- Your future self (freedom to make choices based on values, not finances)

Our Debt Elimination Team:

- Accountability partner: ________________________________
- Support person for tough days: ________________________________
- Person who will celebrate milestones with you: ________________________________

S -Situation After Debt Freedom

What will your life look like when you're debt-free?

Financially:

- Extra $_______ per month for savings and investing
- Ability to handle emergencies without borrowing
- Credit score improvement from paid,off balances
- Foundation for wealth building instead of wealth destroying

Emotionally:

- Relief from constant financial pressure
- Pride in accomplishing a difficult goal
- Confidence that you can handle financial challenges
- Peace of mind about your financial future

Relationally:

- Less money,related stress in your relationships
- Ability to be more generous with others
- Setting positive example for family and friends
- Freedom to make career and life choices based on fulfillment

Practically:

- Options to take risks like entrepreneurship or career changes
- Ability to help family members in emergencies
- Resources to pursue dreams and experiences
- Foundation for building generational wealth

The Debt Elimination Timeline

Phase 1: Stop the Bleeding (Month 1)

Goals:

- No new debt whatsoever
- Identify all current debts and minimum payments
- Create basic plan for debt elimination
- Build first $1,000 emergency fund to avoid new debt

Actions:

- Cut up credit cards or freeze them (literally, in ice)
- List all debts with balances, minimum payments, and interest rates
- Calculate total debt,free timeline
- Find initial extra money for debt payments

Phase 2: Build Momentum (Months 2-6)

Goals:

- Establish consistent debt payment routine
- Pay off first debt completely (psychological win)
- Optimize debt elimination strategy
- Increase income or decrease expenses to speed progress

Actions:

- Apply debt snowball or avalanche method consistently
- Look for ways to increase monthly debt payments
- Celebrate first debt payoff milestone
- Refine strategy based on what's working

Phase 3: Accelerate Progress (Months 7-24)

Goals:

- Maximize debt payments through increased income/decreased spending
- Maintain momentum through inevitable plateaus
- Pay off majority of debt balances
- Prepare for debt,free financial planning

Actions:

- Apply windfalls (tax refunds, bonuses, gifts) directly to debt
- Consider side hustles or income increases specifically for debt payments
- Negotiate with creditors for payoff settlements if appropriate
- Begin planning for post,debt financial goals

Phase 4: Cross the Finish Line (Final months)

Goals:

- Pay off final debts completely
- Celebrate debt,free achievement
- Redirect former debt payments to wealth building
- Help others with similar debt struggles

Actions:

- Make final debt payments
- Update credit reports and celebrate improved credit score
- Begin investing former debt payment amounts
- Share your success story to help others

Common Debt Elimination Obstacles

"I Don't Make Enough Money"

Reality Check: Income is rarely the core problem. Most debt problems stem from spending habits and lack of emergency funds, not insufficient income.

CHAOS Response:

- C: Change habits that create expenses (convenience spending, lack of planning)
- H: Build habits that stretch income (meal planning, generic brands, comparison shopping)
- A: Work toward increasing income while optimizing current income
- O: Get family support for lifestyle changes that reduce expenses
- S: Create situation where your income and expenses align properly

"I Keep Having Emergencies"

Reality Check: Life includes unexpected expenses. If you don't plan for them, they'll always derail your debt progress.

CHAOS Response:

- C: Change the habit of using credit for emergencies
- H: Build habit of saving for emergencies before they happen
- A: Advance toward larger emergency fund even while paying off debt
- O: Get family/support network to help during actual emergencies
- S: Create situation where emergencies don't destroy your financial progress

"It's Going to Take Forever"

Reality Check: It took years to accumulate this debt. It will take time to eliminate it. But "forever" is what happens if you don't start.

CHAOS Response:

- Focus on progress, not perfection
- Celebrate small wins to maintain motivation
- Look for ways to accelerate progress without burnout
- Remember that debt,free is a permanent improvement, not temporary sacrifice

Your Debt CHAOS Action Plan

This Week:

1. List all debts with current balances, minimum payments, and interest rates
2. Choose debt elimination strategy (snowball, avalanche, or hybrid)
3. Identify first debt,creating habit to change
4. Set up first new debt,fighting habit

This Month:

1. Pay first extra payment toward chosen debt
2. Build $1,000 emergency fund to prevent new debt
3. Identify accountability partner and support team
4. Calculate and visualize your debt,free date

This Quarter:

1. Pay off first debt completely (if using snowball method)
2. Increase monthly debt payments if possible
3. Review and optimize strategy based on progress
4. Celebrate progress and recommit to the plan

Debt Freedom Declaration

I am committed to becoming debt-free by [date] ________________.

I will change these habits that create debt:

1. ____
2. ____

I will build these habits that eliminate debt:

1. ____
2. ____

My debt elimination strategy is: ____________________________________

My support team includes: ____________________________________

When I am debt-free, I will: ____________________________________

SUMMARY:

• Debt costs you far more than just interest—it steals options, opportunities, and peace of mind

•CHAOS applied to debt means changing debt,creating habits and building debt,fighting habits

• Choose a debt elimination strategy (snowball, avalanche, or hybrid) and stick with it consistently

• Build emergency fund while paying off debt to prevent new debt creation • Your debt,free situation benefits everyone in your life, not just you

• Focus on progress and celebrate wins to maintain motivation through the process

Your Next Step: Complete your Debt **CHAOS** Action Plan above. This week, list all your debts and make your first extra payment toward debt elimination, even if it's only $25.

Chapter 14: Career , Building Your Financial Foundation

Your Career IS Your Financial Strategy

Here's an uncomfortable truth most financial advice ignores: If you're using credit to pay for basic living expenses, you don't have a spending problem,you have an income problem.

You can cut expenses only so much. You can eliminate the daily coffee, cancel subscriptions, and shop at thrift stores, but if your income doesn't support your basic needs plus some savings, you're just managing poverty instead of building wealth.

Your career isn't separate from your financial strategy, it IS your financial strategy. Everything else (budgeting, investing, debt elimination) is just optimization around the foundation of your earning capacity.

The Career-Finance Connection

Traditional Thinking: "I need to get better at managing money." CHAOS Thinking: "I need to get better at earning money AND managing it strategically."

Most people accept their income as fixed and try to squeeze their lifestyle around it. But your income is actually the most controllable part of your financial equation. It just requires a different set of skills than budgeting.

The Career Leverage Effect:

- A 10% increase in income has more impact than 10% reduction in expenses
- Income increases can compound over time through promotions and career advancement
- Higher income gives you more margin for both mistakes and opportunities
- Income optimization builds wealth faster than expense optimization alone

Applying CHAOS to Career Advancement

C - Changing Your Career-Limiting Habits

Common Career-Limiting Habits:

- Staying in your comfort zone instead of seeking growth opportunities
- Focusing on tasks instead of results and impact
- Avoiding difficult conversations about performance and compensation
- Networking only when you need something instead of building ongoing relationships
- Learning only what's required instead of staying ahead of industry trends
- Competing with colleagues instead of collaborating and lifting others up
- Making yourself indispensable in your current role instead of promotable to the next level

Career Advancement Habit Changes:

Old Habit: Complete assigned tasks (action) → Feel productive (reward) New Habit: Complete tasks + identify process improvements (action) → Feel valuable and get recognized for initiative (reward)

Old Habit: Annual review comes up (trigger) → Hope for the best (action) → Accept whatever increase is offered (reward) New Habit: Quarterly self,evaluation (trigger) → Document achievements and prepare advancement case (action) → Proactive career control (reward)

Your Career-Limiting Habits to Change:

1. ______________________________
2. ______________________________
3. ______________________________

H -Habits That Build Career Capital

Daily Career-Building Habits:

- Arrive early or stay late to work on high,impact projects
- Learn one new industry,relevant skill or concept
- Help a colleague or contribute to team success beyond your job description

- Document your achievements and impact in a career journal

Weekly Career,Building Habits:

- Reach out to one person in your professional network
- Read industry publications or take online courses
- Identify and work on one process improvement in your role
- Seek feedback from supervisors or colleagues on your performance

Monthly Career-Building Habits:

- Have career development conversations with your manager
- Apply for stretch assignments or volunteer for challenging projects
- Update your resume and LinkedIn profile with recent achievements
- Research salary ranges and advancement paths in your field

Quarterly Career,Building Habits:

- Conduct formal self,evaluation and career planning session
- Set up informational interviews with people in roles you want
- Apply for new positions if current role isn't advancing your goals
- Invest in professional development courses or certifications

Your New Career-Building Habits:

1. ____________________
2. ____________________
3. ____________________

A -Advancing Your Income and Opportunities

The Three Paths of Career Advancement:

Path 1: Advancement in Current Company

Strategy: Become indispensable, then promotable

Tactics:

- Excel in current role while learning skills needed for next level
- Build relationships across departments, not just your immediate team
- Solve problems that others avoid or can't handle
- Mentor others and contribute to company culture
- Propose and lead initiatives that save money or generate revenue

Timeline: Usually 12-24 months for meaningful advancement

Path 2: Strategic Job Changes

Strategy: Leverage external opportunities to accelerate advancement

Tactics:

- Research market rates for your skills and experience
- Build relationships with recruiters in your industry
- Develop portable skills that transfer across companies
- Time job searches when you have leverage (good performance, market demand)
- Negotiate not just salary but also title, responsibilities, and growth opportunities

Timeline: Can achieve 20,30% income increases with strategic moves

Path 3: Skill Premium Development

Strategy: Develop rare or highly valuable skills that command premium compensation

Tactics:

- Identify emerging trends in your industry before they become mainstream
- Build expertise at the intersection of multiple disciplines
- Develop leadership and communication skills that complement technical abilities

- Create intellectual property, thought leadership, or recognition in your field
- Build skills that scale (can impact larger organizations or markets)

Timeline: 2-5 years to develop truly premium skill sets

Your Career Advancement Strategy: Current income: $__________ Target income in 2 years: $__________ Strategy chosen: __________________ Key skills to develop: __________________ Next advancement step: __________________

O - Our Career Success

Who benefits when you advance your career?

- Your family (higher income, better benefits, more security)
- Your colleagues (you become someone who helps others advance)
- Your company (you contribute more value and help others develop)
- Your industry (you raise standards and help others succeed)
- Your community (higher income means more resources to contribute)

Our Career Development Team:

- Professional mentor: ________________________________
- Accountability partner: ________________________________
- Industry network contacts: ________________________________
- Skills development support: ________________________________

S -Situation of Career Fulfillment

What does career success look like for you?

Financial Goals:

- Income level that supports your lifestyle and savings goals
- Benefits package that protects your family's security
- Career stability that allows for long,term planning

- Growth trajectory that builds wealth over time

Fulfillment Goals:

- Work that aligns with your values and interests
- Opportunities to use your strengths and develop new capabilities
- Positive relationships with colleagues and leadership
- Balance between work demands and personal life

Impact Goals:

- Contributing to something larger than yourself
- Helping others succeed and grow
- Creating value for customers, clients, or communities
- Building skills and expertise that last beyond any single job

The Income Optimization Framework

Level 1: Maximize Current Role (0-6 months)

Goal: Extract maximum value from your current position

Actions:

- Negotiate salary increase based on market research and performance
- Optimize benefits selection for maximum financial value
- Identify and pursue available advancement opportunities
- Build relationships that could lead to referrals or recommendations

Level 2: Strategic Position Building (6-18 months)

Goal: Position yourself for significant advancement

Actions:

- Develop skills needed for target roles
- Build track record of measurable achievements
- Expand professional network strategically

- Begin exploring external opportunities while excelling in current role

Level 3: Career Leverage Creation (18-36 months)

Goal: Create multiple options and negotiation leverage

Actions:

- Build reputation as expert or leader in your field
- Develop multiple income streams if appropriate
- Create intellectual property or thought leadership
- Mentor others and build influence in your industry

Common Career Advancement Obstacles

"I Don't Have Time to Work on Career Development"

Reality Check: You don't have time NOT to work on career development. Career stagnation is expensive over time.

CHAOS Response:

- C: Change habit of only thinking about career during annual reviews
- H: Build daily/weekly career habits that take minimal time but compound
- A: Advance by making career development part of your work, not separate from it
- O: Get family support for time invested in career growth
- S: Create situation where career growth is integrated into daily life

"My Company Doesn't Promote People"

Reality Check: Some companies truly offer limited advancement. But many people assume limited advancement without actually testing the system.

CHAOS Response:

- Document your value and formally request advancement
- If truly limited, use current role as stepping stone to better opportunity
- Develop portable skills while collecting paycheck

- Build external network for eventual strategic move

"I'm Not Qualified for Higher,Level Roles"

Reality Check: Qualifications can be built. Most successful people felt unqualified before they became qualified.

CHAOS Response:

- Identify specific skill gaps and create development plan
- Seek stretch assignments that build needed experience
- Find mentors who can guide your development
- Remember that confidence and capability develop through action, not just preparation

The Side Hustle Strategy

When to Consider Side Income:

- Current job has limited growth potential
- You want to test entrepreneurial ideas while maintaining stability
- Industry is volatile and you need income diversification
- You have skills or knowledge that could generate additional revenue

Types of Side Income:

- Skill,based: Consulting, freelancing, teaching what you already know
- Time,based: Part,time work, gig economy, service,based business
- Asset,based: Rental income, investing, creating intellectual property
- Passion,based: Monetizing hobbies or interests

Side Hustle Success Principles:

- Start small and test market demand before major investment
- Choose side income that builds skills relevant to your main career
- Set boundaries to prevent side work from damaging primary job performance

- Reinvest early profits to build the side income into meaningful revenue stream

Your Career CHAOS Action Plan

This Month:

1. Research current market salary for your role and experience level
2. Document your achievements and quantify your impact in current role
3. Identify one career,building habit to implement daily
4. Reach out to one person who could provide career guidance or mentorship

This Quarter:

1. Have career development conversation with your manager
2. Apply for one stretch assignment or challenging project
3. Begin developing one key skill needed for your target advancement
4. Update resume, LinkedIn profile, and professional portfolio

This Year:

1. Negotiate salary increase or promotion based on performance and market research
2. Complete meaningful professional development (course, certification, conference)
3. Build relationships with 5-10 new professional contacts
4. Create backup plan (external opportunities) in case current company advancement is limited

Career Success Metrics

Leading Indicators (Things You Control):

- Hours per week invested in career development
- Number of new professional relationships built
- Skills developed and certifications earned

- Quality and quantity of measurable achievements

Lagging Indicators (Results of Your Efforts):

- Salary and total compensation growth
- Advancement opportunities offered
- Recognition and reputation in your field
- Job satisfaction and work,life balance

Your Career Declaration

My target income within 2 years is: $___________________

The career advancement strategy I will pursue is:

____

The career-limiting habits I will change are:

1. ____
2. ____

The career-building habits I will develop are:

1. ____
2. ____

My career development team includes:

____

Success will look like:

____

SUMMARY:

- Your career is your financial foundation—income problems require income solutions
- Career advancement requires changing limiting habits and building career capital systematically
- Three paths exist: advancement in current company, strategic job changes, and skill premium development
- Career development benefits everyone in your life, not just you
- Consistent investment in career growth compounds over time like financial investments
- Success requires both advancing in your current role and creating external opportunities

Your Next Step: Complete your Career **CHAOS** Action Plan above. This week, research the market salary for your role and schedule a career development conversation with your manager or mentor.

Chapter 15: Money - Mastering Your Financial Flow

Money: The Ultimate Tool

Money itself isn't the problem or the solution,it's simply a tool. Like any tool, money can build or destroy, create or waste, advance or hinder your situation depending on how skillfully you use it.

Most people treat money like a mysterious force that controls their lives. They feel like money "disappears," like they "can't hang onto it," or like there's "never enough." But money doesn't have agency, you do.

When you master your financial flow, how money comes in, how it's allocated, and how it goes out, you transform from someone who hopes money works out to someone who makes money work for you.

The Financial Flow System

Think of your finances as a river system:

- Income is the water flowing into your system
- Expenses are the channels where water flows out
- Savings is the reservoir you build for future use
- Investments are systems that create new water sources
- Debt is water flowing backwards, working against your system

Most people have leaky, inefficient financial flow systems. They don't know where all their water is going, they have no reservoirs for dry seasons, and they're constantly stressed about whether there will be enough.

Applying CHAOS to Money Management

C - Changing Your Money,Wasting Habits

Common Money,Wasting Habits:

- Unconscious spending on small items that add up over time
- Emotional spending as response to stress, boredom, or celebration

- Convenience spending to avoid planning or preparation
- Social spending to maintain appearances or avoid difficult conversations
- Procrastination spending (paying late fees, rush charges, premium prices)
- Lifestyle inflation (spending increases automatically when income increases)

Money Flow Habit Changes:

Old Habit: Bored/stressed (trigger) → Browse online and make purchases (action) → Temporary distraction (reward) New Habit: Bored/stressed (trigger) → Check savings account balance and visualize goals (action) → Pride and motivation (reward)

Old Habit: Payday arrives (trigger) → Spend more freely without tracking (action) → Feeling temporarily wealthy (reward) New Habit: Payday arrives (trigger) → Immediately allocate money to categories/goals (action) → Control and intentionality (reward)

Your Money,Wasting Habits to Change:

1. ______________________________
2. ______________________________
3. ______________________________

H - Habits That Optimize Money Flow

Daily Money Management Habits:

- Check account balances every morning (builds awareness)
- Record all expenses in real time (builds consciousness)
- Ask "Does this purchase advance my situation?" before spending
- Transfer any leftover daily money to savings at end of day

Weekly Money Management Habits:

- Review week's spending and identify patterns
- Plan upcoming week's expenses and set spending intentions

- Calculate progress toward monthly and yearly financial goals
- Find one area to optimize spending for the following week

Monthly Money Management Habits:

- Complete comprehensive review of all income and expenses
- Reconcile actual spending with planned spending
- Adjust following month's plan based on lessons learned
- Celebrate any progress toward financial goals

Quarterly Money Management Habits:

- Analyze trends and patterns in your financial flow over 3 months
- Optimize financial systems and tools for better efficiency
- Research better options for banking, insurance, and major expenses
- Plan major purchases or financial moves for upcoming quarter

Your New Money Management Habits:

1. ____
2. ____
3. ____

A - Advancing Your Financial Position

The Four Pillars of Financial Advancement:

Pillar 1: Income Optimization

Current Income Analysis:

- Primary income: $__________ per month
- Secondary income: $__________ per month
- Passive income: $__________ per month
- Total monthly income: $__________

Income Advancement Strategies:

- Negotiate raises and promotions in primary job
- Develop skills that command higher compensation
- Create secondary income streams
- Build passive income through investments

Pillar 2: Expense Optimization

Fixed Expenses (Same every month):

- Housing: $___________
- Transportation: $___________
- Insurance: $___________
- Debt payments: $___________
- Total fixed: $___________

Variable Expenses (Changes monthly):

- Food: $___________
- Utilities: $___________
- Entertainment: $___________
- Personal: $___________
- Total variable: $___________

Expense Optimization Strategies:

- Negotiate better rates on fixed expenses
- Find alternatives that provide same value for less money
- Eliminate expenses that don't align with your values or goals
- Automate good financial choices to reduce decision fatigue

Pillar 3: Savings Acceleration

Current Savings Rate: _________% of income

Savings Allocation Strategy:

- Emergency fund: $__________ (goal: 3,6 months expenses)
- Short,term goals: $__________ (1,2 year goals)
- Long,term goals: $__________ (5+ year goals)
- Total monthly savings: $__________

Savings Acceleration Tactics:

- Automate savings transfers on payday
- Save windfalls (tax refunds, bonuses, gifts) before spending
- Use apps that round up purchases and save the change
- Challenge yourself to beat previous month's savings amount

Pillar 4: Investment Building

Investment Categories:

- Retirement accounts: $__________ per month
- Taxable investments: $__________ per month
- Real estate: $__________ per month
- Business/side hustles: $__________ per month

O -Our Financial Security

Who benefits when you master money management?

- Your spouse/partner (reduced financial stress, shared goals achievement)
- Your children (financial security, positive money modeling, educational opportunities)
- Your extended family (ability to help during emergencies, generous gift,giving)
- Your community (ability to support causes and organizations you care about)
- Your future self (compound growth of good financial habits over decades)

Our Money Management Team:

- Budget accountability partner: ___________________________________
- Financial planning support: ___________________________________
- Emergency contact for major financial decisions: ___________________________________

S - Situation of Financial Flow Mastery

What does financial flow mastery look like?

Daily Experience:

- You check account balances without anxiety
- You make spending decisions confidently based on your plan
- You feel in control of your money instead of controlled by it
- You sleep well without worrying about financial problems

Monthly Experience:

- You pay all bills on time without stress
- You save money consistently toward your goals
- You have margin for unexpected expenses or opportunities
- You make financial decisions based on values, not just affordability

Annual Experience:

- Your net worth grows consistently year over year
- You achieve major financial milestones on schedule
- You can be generous with others without compromising your security
- You feel confident about your long,term financial future

The Money Management System

Level 1: Financial Awareness (Month 1)

Goal: Know where your money actually goes

Tools:

- Banking app or financial tracking tool (Mint, YNAB, Personal Capital)
- Simple expense tracking method (app, spreadsheet, or notebook)
- Weekly money review ritual

Success Metrics:

- You can tell me your account balance without looking
- You know how much you spent on each category last month
- You catch financial mistakes or fraud quickly

Level 2: Intentional Flow (Months 2-3)

Goal: Direct money toward your priorities before spending on everything else

Tools:

- Zero-based budget or percentage,based allocation system
- Automatic transfers to savings and investment accounts
- Envelope method (physical or digital) for variable expenses

Success Metrics:

- You allocate money to goals before spending on wants
- Your actual spending matches your intended spending 80% of the time
- You're consistently saving at least 10% of your income

Level 3: Optimized Systems (Months 4-6)

Goal: Build financial systems that work automatically and efficiently

Tools:

- Optimized banking setup with multiple targeted accounts
- Automatic bill pay for all fixed expenses
- Investment accounts with automatic contributions
- Annual review and optimization of all financial services

Success Metrics:

- Most of your financial management happens automatically
- You spend less than 2 hours per month on money management tasks
- You consistently achieve your monthly financial goals

Level 4: Wealth Building (Months 7+)

Goal: Focus on growing wealth rather than just managing expenses

Tools:

- Investment portfolio suited to your timeline and risk tolerance
- Multiple income streams and passive income development
- Tax optimization strategies
- Estate planning and wealth protection tools

Success Metrics:

- Your net worth grows faster than your income
- You have multiple sources of income
- You're building generational wealth, not just personal security

Common Money Management Obstacles

"I Don't Make Enough Money to Save"

Reality Check: If you truly don't make enough for basic needs, this is an income problem that requires career focus. But most people can find some amount to save.

CHAOS Response:

- Start with saving $1 per day ($365/year)
- Look for the smallest expenses to eliminate first
- Focus simultaneously on increasing income
- Remember that building the saving habit matters more than the initial amount

"I've Tried Budgeting Before and Failed"

Reality Check: Most people fail at budgeting because they try to control every dollar instead of controlling the important dollars.

CHAOS Response:

- Start with 50/30/20 rule: 50% needs, 30% wants, 20% savings/debt
- Automate the important stuff (savings, bills) and be flexible with the rest
- Focus on tracking and awareness before trying to restrict spending
- Adjust the system to work with your personality, not against it

"Unexpected Expenses Always Derail My Plan"

Reality Check: "Unexpected" expenses are actually predictable. Cars need maintenance, medical issues arise, home repairs happen.

CHAOS Response:

- Build emergency fund as your first financial priority
- Create sinking funds for predictable irregular expenses
- Expect your budget to be imperfect and plan for adjustments
- Focus on overall progress, not perfect monthly execution

The Money Flow Assessment

Current Financial Flow Analysis:

Monthly Income: $__________ Monthly Fixed Expenses: $__________ Monthly Variable Expenses: $__________ Monthly Savings: $__________ Monthly Debt Payments: $__________

Financial Flow Health Check:

- Savings rate: ________% (Goal: 10,20%)
- Debt,to,income ratio: ________% (Goal: <36%)
- Emergency fund: $__________ (Goal: 3,6 months expenses)
- Investment rate: ________% (Goal: 10,15% for retirement)

Your Money Flow Optimization Plan:

Biggest money leak to plug: ____________________________ Easiest savings opportunity: ____________________________ Most important financial habit to build: ____________________________ Target savings rate within 6 months: ________%

Your Money CHAOS Action Plan

This Week:

1. Track every expense for 7 days to identify your money flow patterns
2. Set up automatic transfer of $25/week to a separate savings account
3. Identify your biggest money,wasting habit and plan replacement
4. Calculate your current savings rate and set improvement target

This Month:

1. Create simple budget or allocation system for your income
2. Automate savings and bill payments to remove decision fatigue
3. Find $100/month in expenses to eliminate or optimize
4. Build first $1,000 of emergency fund

This Quarter:

1. Achieve consistent 10%+ savings rate
2. Optimize all major expenses (housing, transportation, insurance)
3. Build full 3,month emergency fund
4. Begin investing surplus beyond emergency fund

Money Mastery Declaration

My target monthly savings rate is: ________%

The money-wasting habits I will change are:

1. ____________________________
2. ____________________________

The money management habits I will build are:

1. ______________________________

2. ______________________________

My money management system will be:

____

My financial flow will advance our situation by:

____

SUMMARY:

• Money is a tool that responds to skillful management, not a force that controls your life • Financial flow mastery requires changing money,wasting habits and building money,optimizing habits

• Four pillars of advancement: income optimization, expense optimization, savings acceleration, and investment building • Systems and automation make good financial choices easier and more consistent

• Money management serves your larger life goals, not the reverse • Financial security benefits everyone in your life and enables generosity toward others

Your Next Step: Complete your Money Flow Assessment above and begin tracking all expenses for one week. Set up your first automatic savings transfer of $25/week, even if you think you can't afford it. The habit matters more than the amount initially.

Chapter 16: Emotions and Relationships - The Hidden Forces in Your Financial Life

The Invisible Financial Forces

Money decisions aren't made in a vacuum. Every financial choice you make is influenced by emotions you're feeling, relationships you're managing, and psychological patterns you may not even recognize.

You might think you overspent because you "lack discipline," but the real reason could be that you were feeling inadequate after a difficult conversation with your boss, and buying something made you feel temporarily in control. You might think you "can't save money," but the real issue could be that saving feels like depriving yourself of the only pleasures that help you cope with stress.

Until you understand the emotional and relational forces driving your financial decisions, you'll keep fighting the symptoms instead of addressing the causes. It's like trying to bail water out of a boat without fixing the hole.

The Emotional Spending Cycle

Most financial problems follow predictable emotional patterns:

The Trigger: Something happens that creates emotional discomfort

- Work stress or relationship conflict
- Feeling inadequate compared to others
- Boredom or loneliness
- Celebration or achievement
- Anxiety about the future

The Financial Response: You use money to manage the emotion

- Shopping to feel in control
- Expensive experiences to feel worthy
- Generous spending to feel loved or appreciated
- Impulse purchases to feel excitement

- Avoiding financial tasks to avoid anxiety

The Temporary Relief: The financial response briefly improves your emotional state

- New purchases create temporary excitement
- Expensive experiences provide momentary escape
- Generous spending generates appreciation from others
- Avoided tasks stop causing immediate anxiety

The Emotional Crash: Reality returns, often worse than before

- Guilt about overspending
- Anxiety about financial consequences
- Shame about lack of control
- Frustration about repeated patterns

The Cycle Repeats: Emotional crash creates new triggers, leading to more financial responses

Applying CHAOS to Emotional and Relationship Money Patterns

C - Changing Your Emotional Money Habits

Common Emotional Money Triggers:

Stress Response Spending

- Trigger: High work pressure, family conflict, or overwhelming responsibilities
- Pattern: Shopping, dining out, or expensive convenience purchases for "relief"
- Real Need: Stress management and emotional regulation skills

Inadequacy Compensation Spending

- Trigger: Social comparison, criticism, or feeling "less than" others
- Pattern: Buying status items, expensive experiences, or lifestyle upgrades

- Real Need: Self,worth validation that doesn't depend on external markers

Boredom/Depression Spending

- Trigger: Lack of meaningful engagement or low mood
- Pattern: Impulse purchases, entertainment spending, or "retail therapy"
- Real Need: Purpose, connection, and activities that create genuine fulfillment

Social Pressure Spending

- Trigger: Events, invitations, or expectations from others
- Pattern: Going along with expensive plans to avoid social discomfort
- Real Need: Authentic relationships and communication skills

Habit Replacement Strategies:

Old Pattern: Feel stressed (trigger) → Buy something online (action) → Temporary relief (reward) New Pattern: Feel stressed (trigger) → Take 10,minute walk and call supportive friend (action) → Real relief plus connection (reward)

Old Pattern: Feel inadequate (trigger) → Make expensive purchase to feel better (action) → Temporary confidence boost (reward) New Pattern: Feel inadequate (trigger) → Review personal achievements and progress toward goals (action) → Genuine confidence based on real accomplishments (reward)

Your Emotional Money Patterns to Change:

1. Trigger: ____________________ Pattern: ____________________
2. Trigger: ____________________ Pattern: ____________________
3. Trigger: ____________________ Pattern: ____________________

H -Habits That Build Emotional Financial Strength

Daily Emotional Awareness Habits:

- Check in with your emotional state before making any purchase over $25
- Ask "What am I really trying to accomplish with this purchase?"

- Practice 24,hour delay for any emotional purchase
- End each day by journaling about emotional triggers and financial responses

Weekly Emotional Processing Habits:

- Review the week's spending for emotional patterns
- Identify situations that triggered financial stress or poor decisions
- Plan emotional coping strategies for anticipated challenging situations
- Practice one non,financial activity that provides genuine stress relief

Monthly Relationship and Money Habits:

- Have honest money conversations with spouse/partner about goals and challenges
- Review social spending and assess alignment with personal values
- Evaluate relationships that encourage poor financial habits
- Strengthen relationships with people who support your financial goals

Quarterly Emotional Financial Review:

- Analyze major emotional spending patterns over 3 months
- Assess progress in separating emotions from financial decisions
- Plan personal development activities that address root emotional triggers
- Celebrate growth in emotional financial intelligence

Your New Emotional Financial Habits:

1. ______________________________
2. ______________________________
3. ______________________________

A -Advancing Your Emotional Financial Intelligence

Level 1: Recognition Learning to identify emotional triggers before they lead to financial decisions.

Skills to Develop:

- Emotional awareness and labeling
- Recognition of physical stress signals
- Understanding personal trigger patterns
- Distinguishing between needs and wants in emotional moments

Level 2: Pause and Process Creating space between emotional triggers and financial responses.

Skills to Develop:

- Delayed gratification techniques
- Stress management and emotional regulation
- Alternative coping mechanisms for common triggers
- Decision,making frameworks for emotional moments

Level 3: Healthy Response Systems Building positive ways to meet emotional needs without financial consequences.

Skills to Develop:

- Non,financial stress relief activities
- Healthy relationship communication
- Self,worth validation that doesn't require spending
- Problem,solving skills for underlying issues causing emotional triggers

Level 4: Integration and Teaching Helping others develop emotional financial intelligence while maintaining your own growth.

Skills to Develop:

- Mentoring others in emotional financial growth
- Creating family systems that support healthy money relationships
- Building community around values,based financial decisions
- Modeling integrated emotional and financial health

O - Our Emotional and Relational Financial Health

How Emotional Financial Health Benefits Others:

Your Spouse/Partner:

- Reduced money,related conflict and stress
- More productive financial conversations
- Shared progress toward meaningful goals
- Modeling of healthy emotional regulation

Your Children:

- Healthy money attitudes and habits
- Emotional security about family finances
- Skills for managing their own emotional money relationships
- Example of values,based financial decision making

Your Extended Family:

- Reduced financial strain on family relationships
- Ability to help others without compromising your security
- Positive influence on family money culture
- Emotional availability for relationships not stressed by money problems

Your Community:

- Contribution to causes and organizations you value
- Economic participation that supports local businesses
- Modeling of financial responsibility and emotional health
- Resources to help others in need

S -Situation of Integrated Emotional and Financial Health

What does emotional financial integration look like?

Daily Experience:

- Money decisions align with your values, not your momentary emotions
- Financial choices enhance rather than complicate your relationships
- You feel calm and confident about money even during stressful periods
- Your financial habits support your emotional wellbeing instead of undermining it

Relational Experience:

- Money conversations with loved ones are productive and connecting
- Financial stress doesn't dominate or damage important relationships
- You can be generous with others without compromising your security
- Your financial choices reflect care for others' wellbeing as well as your own

Personal Growth Experience:

- Money becomes a tool for living your values rather than avoiding emotions
- Financial challenges become growth opportunities rather than sources of shame
- You help others develop healthy money relationships
- Your relationship with money supports your overall life satisfaction

Relationship Money Dynamics

Common Relationship Money Patterns:

The Money Avoider and Money Worrier

- One partner avoids financial discussions and decisions
- Other partner carries all financial stress and responsibility
- Result: Resentment builds on both sides, financial problems get worse

The Spender and Saver

- One partner values experiences and immediate gratification

- Other partner prioritizes security and future planning
- Result: Constant conflict over financial priorities and decisions

The Controller and Controlled

- One partner makes all financial decisions
- Other partner feels excluded and infantilized
- Result: Power imbalance damages relationship and financial effectiveness

The Conflict Avoiders

- Both partners avoid discussing money to prevent arguments
- Financial decisions are made individually without coordination
- Result: No shared financial direction, conflicting goals, hidden financial problems

Building Healthy Relationship Money Dynamics:

Weekly Money Meetings

- 30,minute weekly check,in about finances
- Review previous week's spending and upcoming week's needs
- Address any financial stress or concerns
- Celebrate progress toward shared goals

Monthly Financial Planning Sessions

- Comprehensive review of income, expenses, and goal progress
- Planning for major purchases or financial decisions
- Discussion of any needed adjustments to financial strategy
- Celebration of achievements and problem,solving for challenges

Quarterly Financial Visioning

- Review and update shared financial goals and timeline
- Discuss any changes in values, priorities, or life circumstances

- Plan major financial moves for upcoming quarter
- Align financial decisions with relationship and family goals

Annual Financial Retreat

- Half,day or full,day focused planning session
- Review previous year's financial progress
- Set goals and priorities for coming year
- Address any major financial or relationship issues

Common Emotional Financial Challenges

"I Know I Shouldn't Spend Money When I'm Upset, But I Can't Help It"

Understanding the Pattern: Emotional spending provides real psychological benefits—temporary mood improvement, sense of control, distraction from problems. Your brain has learned this pattern because it works in the short term.

CHAOS Response:

- C: Change the habit by identifying specific emotional triggers
- H: Build alternative habits that provide similar psychological benefits without financial cost
- A: Advance by developing genuine emotional regulation skills
- O: Get support from others who understand emotional spending patterns
- S: Create situation where emotional needs are met through relationships and activities, not purchases

"My Partner and I Always Fight About Money"

Understanding the Pattern: Money arguments are usually about deeper issues—control, security, values, communication patterns. The money is just where these issues become visible.

CHAOS Response:

- C: Change the habit of avoiding financial conversations until crisis points

- H: Build regular financial communication rituals
- A: Advance by addressing underlying relationship dynamics, not just financial disagreements
- O: Get professional help (counselor, financial planner) to facilitate healthy communication
- S: Create situation where money enhances rather than threatens your relationship

"I Feel Guilty About Spending Money on Myself"

Understanding the Pattern: Many people, especially those who grew up with financial scarcity, develop beliefs that spending money on personal needs or wants is selfish or dangerous.

CHAOS Response:

- C: Change beliefs about deserving good things and financial self,care
- H: Build habit of planned, values,based personal spending
- A: Advance by distinguishing between necessary self,care and destructive self,indulgence
- O: Get support from others who model healthy financial self,care
- S: Create situation where taking care of yourself financially enables you to better care for others

Your Emotional Financial Action Plan

Emotional Trigger Identification:

My top 3 emotional spending triggers are:

1. ____
2. ____
3. ____

For each trigger, my alternative response will be:

1. ____

2. ______________________________

3. ______________________________

Relationship Money Improvement:

The biggest money,related relationship challenge in my life is:

____

The conversation I need to have about money is:

____

The person I need to have it with is: ______________________________

I will initiate this conversation by: [date] ______________________________

Emotional Financial Habits:

Daily: ______________________________

Weekly: ______________________________

Monthly: ______________________________

Emotional Financial Integration Declaration

I commit to separating my emotions from my financial decisions by:

____

I commit to improving money,related relationships by:

____

The emotional financial habits I will build are:

1. ______________________________

2. ______________________________

My support system for emotional financial growth includes:

____

Success will look like:

____

SUMMARY:

• Financial decisions are driven by emotions and relationships more than logic or math

• Emotional spending follows predictable cycles that can be interrupted and redirected

• Healthy financial relationships require regular communication and shared goals

• Emotional financial intelligence develops through recognition, processing, healthy responses, and integration

• Your emotional financial health impacts everyone in your life, not just you

• True financial success includes emotional and relational wellbeing, not just numerical achievements

Your Next Step: Complete your Emotional Financial Action Plan above. This week, identify your primary emotional spending trigger and plan one alternative response for the next time it occurs. Schedule one honest money conversation with someone important in your life.

Part 5: Conclusion

"The journey of a thousand miles begins with one step. Your financial transformation begins with one habit. Your new life begins with one choice: to stop accepting where you are and start building where you want to be."

Chapter 17: Your CHAOS Implementation Plan

The Integration Challenge

You now understand the **CHAOS** system:

- Changing habits that hold you back
- Habits that advance your situation
- Advancing with purpose toward your goals
- Our shared success that benefits everyone you care about
- Situation that reflects your values and vision

But understanding a system and implementing it are two different challenges. Knowledge without application is just entertainment. The **CHAOS** system only works when you actually use it consistently on real financial challenges.

The most common mistake people make after learning a new system is trying to change everything at once. They get excited about the possibilities and attempt to overhaul their entire financial life in the first month. This almost always leads to overwhelm, inconsistency, and eventual abandonment of the system.

Instead, you need an implementation strategy that builds momentum through small, consistent wins.

Your **CHAOS** Foundation Assessment

Before building your implementation plan, let's assess where you are right now:

Current Situation Inventory:

Financial Status:

- Monthly income: $__________
- Monthly expenses: $__________
- Total debt: $__________
- Emergency fund: $__________

- Current savings rate: ________%

Biggest Financial Challenges:

1. ______________________________
2. ______________________________
3. ______________________________

Strongest Financial Habits:

1. ______________________________
2. ______________________________
3. ______________________________

Weakest Financial Habits:

1. ______________________________
2. ______________________________
3. ______________________________

Your "Will" Assessment:

What brought you to this book? ______________________________

How long have your financial challenges been building? ____________

What happens if nothing changes in the next year? ________________

How ready are you to make difficult changes? (1-10 scale) _________

Support System Assessment:

Who will support your financial transformation?

- Accountability partner: ______________________________
- Emotional support: ______________________________
- Mentor/guide: ______________________________
- Learning community: ______________________________

Who might resist or undermine your changes?

____

How will you handle resistance? ____________________________________

The **CHAOS** Implementation Timeline

Phase 1: Foundation Building (Weeks 1-4)

Goal: Establish basic financial awareness and one keystone habit

Week 1: Awareness Building

- Track every expense for 7 days
- Check account balances daily
- Calculate your true financial position
- Deliverable: Complete financial situation assessment

Week 2: Habit Selection

- Choose one financial habit to build (start small)
- Set up environmental supports for your new habit
- Begin habit tracking
- Deliverable: Daily habit practice for 7 days straight

Week 3: System Creation

- Set up basic money management system (app, spreadsheet, or simple tracking method)
- Automate one financial decision (savings transfer, bill payment, etc.)
- Deliverable: Functional money tracking and one automated process

Week 4: Support Activation

- Identify and contact your accountability partner
- Have honest money conversation with spouse/partner if applicable
- Join one financial community or support group

- Deliverable: Active support system for your financial changes

Phase 2: Momentum Building (Weeks 5-12)

Goal: Build consistency with core habits and begin seeing measurable progress

Financial Habit Stack: Build 3,4 daily/weekly habits that compound

- Daily: Morning financial check,in and evening expense recording
- Weekly: Financial planning session and progress review
- Monthly: Comprehensive financial analysis and goal adjustment

One Major Challenge Focus: Choose your biggest financial challenge and apply full **CHAOS** system

- If debt: Implement debt elimination strategy with specific monthly targets
- If income: Launch career advancement plan with measurable actions
- If expenses: Optimize spending with specific reduction goals
- If savings: Build emergency fund with automated contributions

Relationship Integration: Include important people in your financial transformation

- Regular money meetings with spouse/partner
- Family conversations about shared financial goals
- Social boundary setting with friends who encourage poor financial habits

Phase 3: Acceleration (Weeks 13-24)

Goal: Optimize systems, accelerate progress, and build advanced capabilities

System Optimization:

- Streamline and automate financial management processes
- Optimize income through raises, job changes, or side income
- Optimize expenses through better deals and lifestyle efficiency
- Optimize investments and long,term wealth building

Advanced Habit Building:

- Financial education (regular reading, courses, podcasts)
- Network building (professional relationships, mentorship, community leadership)
- Skill development (career advancement, financial literacy, emotional intelligence)

Challenge Expansion:

- Apply CHAOS to additional financial areas beyond your initial focus
- Help others implement similar systems (teaching reinforces learning)
- Plan and execute major financial goals (home purchase, investment portfolio, career change)

Phase 4: Integration and Mastery (Weeks 25-52)

Goal: Achieve financial momentum that sustains itself and enables you to help others

Mastery Indicators:

- Financial habits happen automatically without willpower
- You make financial decisions based on values and long,term goals, not emotions
- You can handle financial setbacks without derailing your progress
- You're advancing toward major life goals with confidence

Leadership Development:

- Mentor others who are beginning their financial transformation
- Contribute to financial wellness in your community
- Build wealth that enables generosity and impact beyond yourself
- Model integrated financial and emotional health for family

Your Personal CHAOS Implementation Plan

Phase 1 Commitments (Next 30 Days):

My one foundational habit will be:

____

When I will do this habit: ______________________________

How I will track this habit: ______________________________

My accountability partner is: ______________________________

How often we will check in: ______________________________

Major Challenge Focus:

My biggest financial challenge is: ______________________________

My CHAOS approach to this challenge:

C -Habit to change: ______________________________

H- Habit to build: ______________________________

A -How this advances my situation: ______________________________

O- Who benefits from solving this: ______________________________

S -What success looks like: ______________________________

Support System Activation:

Money conversation I need to have: ______________________________

With whom: ________________

By when: ________________

Community I will join: ______________________________

Professional help I need: ______________________________

Common Implementation Obstacles and Solutions

Obstacle 1: "I Keep Forgetting to Do My New Habits"

Root Cause: Habit isn't attached to strong existing trigger

CHAOS Solution:

- C: Change approach from willpower,based to trigger,based
- H: Stack new habit onto existing strong habit
- A: Use environmental design to make habit more obvious
- O: Get accountability partner to check on habit consistency
- S: Start with smaller version of habit that's easier to remember

Obstacle 2: "My Family/Friends Don't Support My Changes"

Root Cause: Changes threaten existing relationship dynamics or others' financial insecurities

CHAOS Solution:

- C: Change communication approach to emphasize benefits for them
- H: Build habit of regular, patient conversation about your goals
- A: Find new community that supports your financial transformation
- O: Focus on how your changes benefit everyone in the long run
- S: Accept that some relationships may need boundaries during your transformation

Obstacle 3: "I'm Not Seeing Results Fast Enough"

Root Cause: Unrealistic timeline expectations or focus on lagging indicators instead of leading indicators

CHAOS Solution:

- C: Change focus from results to consistency with process
- H: Track and celebrate process wins (habits completed) not just outcome wins (money saved)
- A: Remember that real transformation takes months/years, not days/weeks
- O: Get encouragement from others who've completed similar transformations

- S: Adjust timeline expectations based on reality of sustainable change

Obstacle 4: "I Had a Setback and Feel Like Starting Over"

Root Cause: All,or,nothing thinking that treats any mistake as complete failure

CHAOS Solution:

- C: Change from perfection thinking to progress thinking
- H: Build habit of quick recovery instead of extended self,punishment
- A: Use setbacks as learning opportunities to strengthen your system
- O: Get support and perspective from your accountability team
- S: Normalize setbacks as part of the transformation process, not evidence of failure

Your CHAOS Success Metrics

Leading Indicators (Things You Control):

☐ Days per week you complete your core financial habits

☐ Number of financial conversations with spouse/partner per month

☐ Hours per month invested in financial education

☐ Weekly check,ins completed with accountability partner

☐ Major financial decisions made using CHAOS framework

Lagging Indicators (Results of Your Efforts):

☐ Monthly increase in net worth

☐ Debt reduction progress toward elimination target

☐ Savings rate improvement over time

☐ Credit score improvement

☐ Achievement of major financial milestones

Life Integration Indicators (How Finances Support Your Life):

☐ Reduced financial stress and anxiety

☐ Improved relationships due to better money management

☐ Increased ability to be generous with others

☐ Progress toward major life goals (home ownership, career change, etc.)

☐ Confidence in your ability to handle financial challenges

The CHAOS Commitment Contract

I commit to implementing the CHAOS system for financial transformation by:

Daily: ____

Weekly: ____

Monthly: ____

I will measure my progress by: ________________________________

My accountability partner is: ________________________________

My target date for Phase 1 completion is: ________________

My major financial goal for this year is:

____

I understand that transformation takes time, and I commit to the process even when progress feels slow.

Signature: ________________ Date: ________________

Your Next Steps

This Week:

1. Complete your CHAOS Foundation Assessment
2. Choose and begin your one foundational habit
3. Set up basic financial tracking system
4. Contact your accountability partner

This Month:

1. Complete Phase 1 of implementation timeline

2. Have important money conversation with spouse/partner/family
3. Apply CHAOS framework to your biggest financial challenge
4. Join community or get professional support if needed

This Quarter:

1. Complete Phase 2 with consistent habits and measurable progress
2. Begin optimizing systems and accelerating progress
3. Help at least one other person with their financial transformation
4. Evaluate and adjust your implementation plan based on lessons learned

The Compound Effect of CHAOS

Remember: small, consistent changes compound over time into extraordinary results.

Daily habits → Weekly progress → Monthly milestones → Quarterly achievements → Annual transformation → Lifetime of financial freedom

Your financial transformation doesn't happen all at once—it happens one choice at a time, one habit at a time, one day at a time.

But when you look back a year from now, you'll be amazed at how far you've traveled by simply putting one foot in front of the other consistently.

SUMMARY:

• Implementation matters more than understanding, knowledge without action is just entertainment

• Start with foundation building, not overwhelming system overhauls

• Use the four,phase timeline to build sustainable momentum over 12 months

• Focus on leading indicators (habits) more than lagging indicators (results)

• Expect and plan for obstacles—they're part of the process, not evidence of failure

• Small, consistent changes compound into extraordinary transformation over time

Your Next Step: Complete your Personal CHAOS Implementation Plan above and begin your foundational habit today. Not tomorrow, not next week—today. Your future self is counting on the choices you make right now.

Chapter 18: Give Yourself Credit for Trying

The Most Important Words You'll Read

Give yourself credit for trying.

Not for succeeding perfectly. Not for having it all figured out. Not for never making mistakes or having setbacks.

Give yourself credit for trying.

For picking up this book when you could have chosen to ignore your financial problems. For reading this far when you could have given up after the first few chapters. For considering change when staying the same would have been easier.

Give yourself credit for trying.

The Courage to Begin Again

You know what took the most courage after Will crashed into my life? It wasn't surviving the physical injuries or dealing with the medical bills. It wasn't even admitting that my financial situation had become broken.

The most courage was required to believe that I could get it all back again and MORE! To believe that someone who I had never met could break me and leave me broken to the extent that I wouldn't rebound, was NOT an option. I had to figure out how to heal and how to build something better.

Every morning when I woke up in pain, broken, and uncertain about the future, I had to make a choice: Give up and accept that this was just how things were going to be, or try again to build something better.

Most days, trying felt impossible. Some days, I chose to give up. But the success came because I chose to try more days than giving up. 1 became 2 and 2 became 4!

And trying, it turns out, is enough.

The Trying Transformation

Here's what I discovered about trying:

Trying creates hope. When you're actively working toward something better, you can imagine a future that's different from your present. Hope isn't naive optimism, it's the realistic belief that your actions can improve your circumstances.

Trying builds capability. Every attempt, successful or not, teaches you something. Every effort, perfect or flawed, builds skills and confidence. You become more capable through trying, even when individual attempts don't succeed.

Trying creates momentum. Motion creates more motion. Action creates more action. When you're trying, you're moving. When you're moving, you're more likely to keep moving.

Trying inspires others. When people see you working to improve your situation, it gives them permission to work on theirs. Your effort to change creates ripples that affect everyone around you.

Trying is the only requirement for transformation. You don't have to be perfect, disciplined, naturally organized, or "good with money." You just have to be willing to keep trying.

What Trying Looks Like

Trying doesn't look like perfection. It looks like this:

You try to stick to your budget, overspend one week, feel terrible about it, and then try again the next week.

You try to save money consistently, have an emergency that wipes out your progress, and then start building your emergency fund again.

You try to change your spending habits, slip back into old patterns during a stressful period, and then recommit to your new approach.

You try to have productive money conversations with your spouse, have a fight about finances instead, and then try a different approach to the conversation.

This is what trying looks like. Not smooth progress toward clear goals, but messy, imperfect, human effort to create something better than what you have now.

The Credit You Deserve

You deserve credit for:

Acknowledging that your current financial situation isn't working. Many people spend their entire lives pretending their financial problems don't exist or will somehow solve themselves.

Seeking solutions instead of just complaining about problems. You could have chosen to blame external circumstances, other people, or bad luck. Instead, you're looking for ways to improve your situation through your own actions.

Investing time and energy in learning new approaches. Reading this book, thinking about your habits, considering changes to your lifestyle—this is work that many people never do.

Being willing to examine your own role in creating your current situation. It takes courage and maturity to look honestly at your own habits and choices instead of just focusing on things outside your control.

Considering changes that might be uncomfortable or difficult. Change is hard. The fact that you're willing to contemplate changing habits, relationships, or lifestyle patterns shows strength and commitment to growth.

The Journey Continues

This book ending doesn't mean your journey is over—it means it's really beginning.

You now have:

- A framework (CHAOS) for organizing your approach to financial improvement
- An understanding of how habits work and how to change them
- Tools and strategies for addressing debt, career, money management, and emotional financial patterns
- A plan for implementing changes systematically over time
- Permission to be imperfect while still making progress

What you do with these tools is up to you.

My Promise to You

I promise you this: If you keep trying, if you keep applying the **CHAOS** system even imperfectly, if you keep getting back up after setbacks and keep working toward the situation you want to create, your finances will improve.

Not immediately. Not without effort. Not without setbacks and challenges.

But they will improve.

More importantly, you will improve. You'll become someone who doesn't accept problems as permanent. You'll become someone who takes responsibility for creating solutions. You'll become someone who helps others believe they can change their situations too.

You'll become someone who tries, and keeps trying, and deserves credit for trying.

Your "Will" Becomes Your "Why"

Remember Will? The drunk driver who crashed into my life and set this whole transformation in motion?

Will most likely never thought he could have destroyed my future. As a matter of fact that asshole probably didn't think about me at all and that's what chaos does. What he actually did was give me the motivation to beat the chaos and rebuild my life stronger than it had ever been before.

Your "Will"—whatever brought you to this book, whatever crisis or dissatisfaction or desire for change motivated you to seek something better—isn't the end of your story. It's the beginning of your transformation.

Your chaos isn't your enemy. It's your raw material.

Your trying isn't failure because it's not perfect. It's the most important thing you can do.

The **CHAOS** Promise, Fulfilled

Remember the promise from Chapter 1?

"What if your financial chaos isn't your enemy, but your greatest untapped resource? The CHAOS system , Changing Habits to Advance Our Situation , transforms financial disorder into organized progress. Whether you're facing a crisis or just tired of money stress controlling your life, CHAOS meets you exactly where you are. You don't need to be perfect, organized, or have it all figured out. You just need to be ready to stop fighting the disorder and start harnessing it."

You now know how to harness your chaos. You have the system. You have the tools. You have the understanding.

What you've always had, and what you need to give yourself credit for, is the willingness to try.

Your Trying Declaration

I give myself credit for:

- Recognizing that my current financial situation needs to change
- Seeking solutions and strategies for improvement
- Being willing to examine and change my own habits
- Investing time and energy in learning new approaches
- Committing to try, even when success isn't guaranteed

I commit to:

- Keep trying, even when progress feels slow
- Give myself credit for effort, not just results
- Get back up after setbacks and keep moving forward
- Help others who are trying to improve their financial situations
- Remember that trying is enough, and trying is everything

I understand that:

- Transformation takes time and isn't always linear

- Setbacks are part of the process, not evidence of failure
- My willingness to try is already changing my situation
- Every attempt teaches me something valuable
- My trying inspires others to try too

The Final CHAOS

Change happens when you try. Habits form when you try consistently. Advancement occurs when you try strategically. Others benefit when you try courageously. Success is inevitable when you try persistently.

Give Yourself Credit

Right now, before you close this book, I want you to do something:

Look back at where you were when you started reading. Look at what you've learned, what you've considered changing, what plans you've made.

Look at the person who was courageous enough to admit their financial situation needed improvement.

Look at the person who was committed enough to invest time in learning new strategies.

Look at the person who cares enough about their future and their family's future to do the hard work of transformation.

Look at the person who is trying.

That person deserves credit.

That person is you.

Give yourself credit for trying.

Now go change your life, one habit at a time, one choice at a time, one day at a time.

Your future self is counting on the person who's willing to try.

And that person is more than enough.

THE END

YOUR NEXT STEP

Reading this book was step one. Now it's time to implement.

★ Repair and rebuild your credit

Visit GiveMeCreditForTrying.com

★ Join the CHAOS community

Visit GiveMeCreditForTrying.com

★ Loved this book? Leave a review on Amazon

Your review helps someone else find their way out of chaos.

"Give yourself credit for trying — then keep going."

— Shelton Marchman

Acknowledgments

To Will, wherever you are: Thank you for the chaos that became my greatest teacher but I still send a GIANT F*** YOU! Maggie and Preston: Thank you for believing in our ability to build something beautiful from the wreckage. I love you both more than I could ever say! To Ava and Max, welcome to the circus! Dadda promises to always keep you on your toes and love you unconditionally.

To everyone who shared their financial struggles with me: Your willingness to be vulnerable made this book possible.

To every reader who chooses to try: Your courage to change your situation changes the world. I TRULY mean these words.

ABOUT THE AUTHOR

Shelton Marchman is a fintech credit strategist, entrepreneur, author, and mindset mentor with over 20 years of experience leading Credit Risk and Receivables operations across multi-million dollar lending portfolios.

He is the creator of the Give Me Credit For Trying system and the founder of Custom Credit Solutions. In these capacities he has helped over 4000 clients rebuild their financial lives and start anew. His work sits at the intersection of financial strategy, systems thinking, and human transformation.

Shelton's personal journey- from near-fatal car accident to financial rock bottom to system founder — is the lived experience behind the CHAOS system and every page of this book. He believes that your most chaotic moment is not your ending. It is your raw material.

He lives by a simple conviction: *give yourself credit for trying, then build from there.*

Connect with Shelton on all social media:

🌐 GiveMeCreditForTrying.com

🌐 CustomCreditSolutions.net

FB Facebook.com/SheltonMarchman

IG: @sheltonmarchmangmcft

Made in United States
Orlando, FL
04 November 2026

90204194R00092